Boundaries in Human Relationships

How to be Separate and Connected

Anné Linden

Crown House Publishing Limited
www.crownhouse.co.uk
www.chpus.com

First published by

Crown House Publishing Ltd
Crown Buildings, Bancyfelin, Carmarthen, Wales, SA33 5ND, UK
www.crownhouse.co.uk

and

Crown House Publishing Company LLC
6 Trowbridge Drive, Suite 5, Bethel, CT 06801-2858, USA
www.CHPUS.com

© Anné Linden 2008

The right of Anné Linden to be identified as the author of this work has
been asserted by her in accordance with the Copyright, Designs and
Patents Act 1988.

British Library Cataloguing-in-Publication Data
A catalogue entry for this book is available
from the British Library.

ISBN 978-184590076-2 (1845900766)

LCCN 2007932739

Printed and bound in the USA

"Sing and dance together and be joyous, but let each one of you be alone
Even as the strings of a lute are alone though they quiver with the same music."

—*The Prophet* by Kahlil Gibran

*Dedicated to Quinn, my Mythic Hounds, and the
Standing People, because you nourish my soul!*

Contents

Acknowledgments

I am awed by and grateful for how much I have learned in the process of writing this book. This book came out of my teaching and now will inform and deepen my teaching—coming full circle!

I want to acknowledge and extend my deepest appreciation and heartfelt thanks to the following people: the colleagues and students in my Assistant Trainers Program for all their help in my research into human boundaries; to my extraordinary teachers, Richard Bandler, John Grinder, and Milton Erickson who each in their own special way opened the path to my mind and creativity; Natalie Koralnik, a student, colleague, and translator extrodinaire (she translated into French my first book, *The Enneagram and NLP*, and this, my third book), who encouraged me for more than two years to write this book; Hélène De Castilla, editor of *Intereditions*, who supported the idea of this book even before it was written; Suz, who is always there with positive feedback and belief in me; Melissa, whose wisdom and depth of spirit never ceases to amaze me; all those students and clients who have responded so enthusiastically to my seminars and therapeutic work based upon this approach to problems and fulfillment; and Peter Skinner, who helped me edit the manuscript. And, last but not least, thanks to Steven Fornal, who with great patience and fortitude has turned my almost illegible handwriting into clean, crisp type.

Introduction

This book explores how human beings remain individuals and yet can empathize and identify with others. It is an exploration of the many facets of individuality and togetherness, and it analyzes the most essential element that either supports or destroys self-esteem and relationships: *boundaries,* or the ability to be *separate and connected.*

I hope to increase the reader's awareness of human boundaries and how we actually "do" them—because boundaries are not accidents of fate or random luck. This book is for the reader who is open to considering relationships and self-esteem from a different perspective. While I do include some exercises to increase the reader's skill at purposefully "doing" boundaries, my primary intention is to provoke thought and questions.

In this book, I draw upon over 25 years of work as a teacher and therapist. I have observed and interacted with many students and clients, most of whom are adult professionals from business, the arts, education, and the helping professions, and many in the midst of either personal or professional transitions. All were motivated to improve themselves, their relationships, and their ability to communicate. This book is also the result of becoming aware of myself, my "stuck" places, traps, strengths, and my relationships with lovers, family, children, colleagues, friends, students, and clients.

I teach human communication and change using Neuro Linguistic Programming, Ericksonian Hypnosis, the Linden Parts Model, and the Linden Boundaries Model. To explain these models, I draw on years of experience and research into what makes for a successful relationship and a functioning, whole, and happy human being. I define "happy" not as deliriously gay, joyful, or ecstatic—but content yet yearning, satisfied but challenged, and moving toward as-yet unrealized dreams while savoring the present moment with all one's senses.

About 20 years ago, boundaries became more than an intellectual, taken-for-granted, little-understood concept when a colleague and I were discussing our work and some recent examples of success and failure. At one moment, she looked at me and said, "Anné, all your work is about boundaries!" Immediately I knew this to be true, but at the same time I really didn't know what it meant. I did not know specifically what human boundaries were, and I certainly did not know *how* they worked—how humans "did" boundaries. I knew for sure that they didn't just happen, so I set out to discover what they were and how human beings create and maintain them.

At the time, I was lucky enough to have a small group of professionals in my Assistant Trainers Program, people with whom I had met four times a month for two years. They were intelligent, highly trained, and motivated professionals who enthusiastically participated in my research into boundaries. With their help over several years, I began to map out the basic structure of the Linden Boundaries Model. Since I am a teacher, this work evolved into trainings through which I further developed and refined the model and process of boundaries. The more I taught, the more I learned! When I began to write this book, I thought I understood boundaries and how they worked. I did, but writing my ideas down forced me to a much deeper level of understanding.

The first five chapters explore the structure of boundaries, what they are, and the patterns upon which they depend. Chapter 1 defines boundaries, loss of boundaries, and walls. There are three levels of boundaries, and Chapters 2, 3, and 4 describe these levels in depth. Chapter 5 lays out the five developmental, psychological patterns that form the foundation of boundaries. Chapter 6 explains the process of boundaries; it provides an in-depth study of how exactly the human being "does" boundaries. It also offers a step-by-step explanation of the three skills (perceptual, physiological, and cognitive) that we use to create and maintain boundaries. Exercises to increase awareness of and strengthen each skill are included at the end of Chapter 6. The last four chapters describe my own and others' personal experiences that will deepen the reader's understanding and recognition of the practical implications of boundaries in the important areas of our lives. They examine how the lack of boundaries or the exaggeration of them into walls influences our relationships, our identity, and our self-esteem.

Anné Linden
January 2008

Chapter I

Boundaries

"How is it possible to be separate and connected?" This chapter describes the function of human boundaries and how they affect this apparent paradox of separation and connection. It examines the meaning of separate and connected; and what happens when the permeability of boundaries becomes so diffuse that there is no longer any separation and, conversely, when separation becomes so calcified that there can be no permeability thus preventing any connection.

I am a smart woman, but sometimes I sputter, repeat myself endlessly, yell, and in general speak with little sign of intelligence or coherence. Why? The answer is not temporary insanity, drunkenness, or senility. It is the loss of boundaries, that intangible distinction between our inner and outer worlds, between ourselves and others.

I call boundaries intangible because you cannot see, hear, touch, smell, or taste them, but they are real and essential to our well-being and functioning in this world. Have you ever considered how you know the difference between your emotions and your mate's, your thoughts and your child's? Do you even recognize that there is a difference, or is the difference so great that you sense a barrier between yourself and the rest of the world?

The French word *frontiere* serves for both boundaries and borders. Borders are those distinctions we make between countries, between where our property ends and our neighbors' begin. Borders are lines drawn on maps, rivers and streets, guard posts with closed gates, fences, walls, hedges, doors. You can see or touch borders; they are what separates countries, property, houses, and offices. "Fences make good neighbors." [Robert Frost, American poet]. What of the distinctions between emotions, thoughts, beliefs, and values? Between you and not you, between you and me?

Remember a time when you came home after a day away, and you felt glad to be back. As you entered the house, your feelings began to change. You started to feel down, but things were okay—you'd had a good day, and there were no dirty dishes in the sink. Then the person you live with came into the room. Her expression was dark, she was unusually quiet, she answered your questions in monosyllables, she was distant, and she stared off into space a lot. When you asked her if something was wrong she replied with a shrug and said "I don't know." You began to feel bad, even depressed. What was going on here? Could it be that you had "caught" your significant other's emotions and felt them as though they were your own? Because of the nature of close relationships, it is easy to lose your boundaries, take on the other's emotions or thoughts, or expect the other person to have the same thoughts or emotions that you have.

Boundaries are those distinctions that we make between ourselves and the world, between ourselves and significant others, and between different types of situations—that is, different contexts. These distinctions create separation and yet are permeable, allowing the exchange of emotions and information. The difference between permeable and solid is similar to that between a sponge and a brick. A sponge absorbs any moisture with which it comes into contact; the moisture passes through the sponge. A brick is not particularly porous, and any moisture it comes into contact with mostly rolls off, having little effect on the brick. Through permeability, human boundaries allow connection and simultaneously create separation. A great example of a boundary is your skin. Think for a moment about how your skin functions: it keeps you separate from the rest of the world and distinguishes you from the world around you. Without skin, much of you would be a puddle on the ground, without even as much form as a shapeshifter. At the same time that your skin is giving you form, it is permeable. It breathes, releasing toxins from your body into the air and taking in oxygen and other external elements. You can put a nicotine patch on your skin, and the nicotine enters your bloodstream. Consider the effect of other topical medications. Because of the permeability of your skin, the external substance is taken into your body. Imagine what it feels like to get something impermeable on your skin, such as oil-based paint or liquid glue. If you don't wash it off, your skin soon begins to itch, become irritated, and eventually would die. Skin has two properties important for boundaries: the ability to separate, to make a distinction between you and the world around you, and permeability, which allows you to connect with the world around you. "(Skin) the limiting membrane that allows the human being to distinguish the difference between me and not me. That is the distinction between external reality and internal reality (including perception of external reality)." [Donald W. Winnicott, noted British pediatrician, child psychoanalyst, teacher, and theorist. 1896–1971]

When this separation becomes too rigid and solid, it becomes a wall, making exchange of experience and connection impossible. When the permeability becomes too diffuse and excessive, there is no separation, and you merge, becoming the other person, nature, judgment or value, taking on the other's emotions. Boundaries are lost.

When you have boundaries, you are separate and connected. As you read these words, do you have a strong response to them? For some people, it is intolerable to be separate; separate means alone, isolated, without the possibility of connection. For others, connection can be threatening or suffocating, signifying a loss of self. The concept of separate *and* connected is a paradox. It seems to convey an inherent contradiction. How can you be connected when you are separate? And how can you be separate when you are connected? As F. Scott Fitzgerald said, "The test of a first-rate intelligence is the ability to hold two opposing ideas in the mind at the same time and still retain the ability to function." Let's examine these words and their meaning.

According to the dictionary, to *separate* means "to make a distinction." The archaic meaning is "to set aside for a special purpose." It could also mean "to sever," "to block off," "to isolate," or "to become detached." *Connect* means "to place or establish in a relationship," "joined or linked together," "having a social, professional or commercial relationship." So is this concept truly contradictory, or is it in fact quite logical? By *separate*, I do not mean to sever, to block off, to isolate, or become detached but rather *to make a distinction*. *Connected* is to be linked, to have a relationship. How can you have a relationship or be linked to someone or something if you are not separate? If there is no distinction between you and the other, who is making the connection?

I have often encountered objections to the idea of being separate, because to some it implies being detached and cut off from others. I propose that if you are *not* separate you *cannot* connect. Connected does *not* mean merged. To merge means to become the other and lose yourself in the other. This state is desirable when making love, bonding with a baby, watching a sunset, or working in your garden. There are many times when you want to merge and become one with the other. This loss of self can be positive and wonderful. The purpose of no boundaries is to give up all distinctions and separation and lose yourself in another, to merge with nature or a situation that is pleasurable. However, as desirable as it may be, it must be done with awareness and choice. Otherwise, we lose our freedom, our uniqueness, ourselves. Every human being is unique and individual, and only with the ability to recognize and choose to "do" boundaries (or not) can you truly know yourself and touch your potential.

Boundaries are not something you must have all the time, but you must know the difference between when you are "doing" boundaries, when you create walls, and when you lose your boundaries. This awareness is essential for your self-esteem and for positive relations with others.

Boundaries enable you to know and understand yourself, including your values and beliefs, as separate and unique from others while still connecting with them. You can then be a part of the world and allow the world to touch you *as* you remain distinct from the world. The purpose of walls is to protect you from the world, from being overwhelmed by the emotions of others or by situations that are physically, mentally, emotionally, or spiritually dangerous.

When I lose my ability to communicate in any kind of rational way, when I sputter and yell, I've lost the distinction between my thoughts and feelings. I've become overwhelmed by my emotions, another person's emotions and thoughts, or the emotions of the situation.

⌒

Once upon a time, there were two very devoted friends, Beatrice and Samantha. They enjoyed spending time together and were always very happy to see each other again after being apart. They were truly best friends. Beatrice thought Samantha was the most beautiful, elegant, and graceful creature she had ever seen, so she decided she wanted to be just like Samantha. She observed her very carefully and tried hard to look and move and sound like Samantha.

It seemed that the harder Beatrice tried, the less she succeeded. She became frustrated, impatient, discouraged, and finally depressed. No matter how much she tried to be like Samantha, she kept failing miserably. She knew it wasn't working, but she couldn't seem to give up her dream of being like Samantha. She'd beat herself up asking, "Why? Why can't I look and be like Samantha? She is so perfect—why can't I be like her?" Nothing seemed to work, and Beatrice felt worse and worse.

After several weeks of failing to become at all like Samantha, Beatrice had a dream. In the dream, she was floating high above the earth on a cloud, and as she floated she looked down and saw a group of Samanthas! You see, Samantha is an Afghan Hound! And as Beatrice watched these elegant, beautiful creatures, she became aware of a movie that described the history of the Afghan Hound unfolding just above this group. Such is the magical nature of dreams. Beatrice learned that Afghan Hounds were bred many, many years ago to hunt with the horsemen of Afghanistan. Thus, they have long, slender bodies and legs that help them cover ground quickly and keep up with the horses over steep, ice-clad mountains. They have a long, plume-like tail to help balance them on the treacherous terrain. Their long, silky hair keeps them warm in the frigid climate and because they are sighthounds—dogs who hunt primarily with their sense of sight—they have large eyes set as wide apart as their narrow skulls allow. Their muzzle and jaw are long and narrow, and because they hunt in packs of 20 to 30, they have plenty of help bringing down and holding their prey. Since they depend upon their eyes to hunt their sense of hearing is secondary; explaining why their ears are long and covered with silky hair. Everything about the Afghan Hound is designed for her mission in life: to hunt with the horsemen in the cold mountains of Afghanistan, and for this she is perfect.

As Beatrice continued to float on her cloud and to dream, she saw another group of dogs—Boxers. It happens that Beatrice is a Boxer, and as she watched this group, a movie of the history of Boxers unfolded above them. Boxers originated in Germany and are members of the working group of dogs. This group's primary mission is to work with humans to help pull sleds, herd, rescue, and protect. The Boxer's mission in life is to protect her human family. Her square body and legs support a wide and muscular chest that enables her to jump easily and use her short, square muzzle and jaw to fight and hold opponents—human or animal. She is short-haired with a short tail, which makes it harder for an enemy to grab hold of her. Since hearing is her most important sense, her ears stand up short and pointy to allow the greatest sensitivity to sound, while her eyes are quite small. Boxers are bred to their mission: incredible strength and power to defend and protect. As such, the Boxer is perfect.

Through this dream, Beatrice begins to realize that both she *and* Samantha are beautiful. They are very different because their mission in life is different but within that purpose each is perfect just the way she is. Beatrice continues to love and admire Samantha and now understands that she is special and beautiful in her own way.

Chapter II

Internal/External Boundaries

At this first and most essential level of boundaries, there are eight categories in which boundaries can be distorted into loss of boundaries or walls:

1. Projection (no boundaries). Isolation (walls)
2. Mode: no boundaries or walls between thinking, feeling, and doing
3. Causality: no boundaries or walls results either in irrational connection or loss of logical connection
4. Generalization: loss of boundaries creates the experience of "part equals the whole"
5. Polarity: walls that result in extremes
6. Threshold: no boundaries or walls leads to the inability to know when enough is enough
7. Identity: no boundaries, merging a discrete external activity with the sense of self
8. Time: no boundaries or walls between past, present, or future, which distorts reality

Once you're "grown up," you know you're not the maple tree in your back yard; and at the movies, you know you're *not* in the front seat of a car with the good guy as he's chased over a cliff by the bad guys. Even though you're holding onto the arms of your seat so hard your fingers are cramping and you're screaming silently, you know you're not in the car—well, afterwards you know you weren't, for a few seconds you *are* in that car!

Internal/external boundaries are the foundation of the three levels of boundaries. These boundaries begin to develop soon after birth, albeit in a primitive and unsophisticated way, and they remain unstable and inconsistent until adulthood. They are the distinctions that you make between your internal world: *me,* and the external world, *not me.* If I'm watching the news of a terrible accident on television and I've set healthy boundaries, I can empathize with the people involved and feel their pain, but I know it's not me or my family that's involved. I'm both separate and connected. If I lose my boundaries, I can't continue to watch. I'm overwhelmed with fear or sadness as though I'm actually involved personally in the accident, that it's happening right now to me or my family. I merge with the victims, and the distinctions between me and the people in the accident become so porous that all separation is lost. If I put up walls to protect myself from the pain of others, I detach, sever myself from the experience, and feel nothing. The separation becomes solid, and I have no connection to the emotions of others. This is the basis of desensitization. During war times, people put up walls to the horrific images of dead bodies, burned villages, and body bags until they feel very little. Walls are a self-protective mechanism against overwhelming emotion.

Limitations and more serious problems only occur when you're not aware that you're losing your boundaries or building walls. These patterns can become habitual or develop into the belief it's *"just how I am."* Awareness means to be conscious of something, to know, to realize what you're doing; *a habit* is a sequence of behavior, thoughts, and feelings that is repeated predictably without conscious awareness when certain stimuli are present in the external world.

Some people respond to strong emotions by putting up walls to protect themselves, while others find comfort or safety in losing boundaries and merging. Both responses can be beneficial or satisfying except when they become habitual and you react the same way no matter what the external circumstances are. Without awareness, you have no choice, and when you have no choice, you'll always do what you've always done and you'll always get what you've always gotten! Habits are based on basic stimulus–response phenomena; something occurs in the external world, and you react automatically. Historically, many habits originate in childhood; when you are young, you don't have dependable boundaries, and your initial responses are probably the result of loss of boundaries or walls. When these responses bring you feelings of pleasure or safety, the connection between an event in the external world and merging or detaching becomes hardwired into your unconscious. The more you do this, the better you get at it! It's the same as rehearsing or practicing something. The association between the stimulus and the response becomes unconscious and automatic.

The response may become limiting or problematic as you get older even though the historic response had a positive effect.

> A little boy of 18 months is sitting in his high chair waiting for his dinner. He is hungry, and he starts to holler and bang his spoon. His father gets a little frazzled and hurries to give him his pasta. Now, as an adult, whenever he doesn't get what he wants when he wants it, he starts to yell and carry on. It's not very useful behavior in a grown-up man, but it's become an automatic response.

> Nell has a second-grade teacher who indicates with certain words, tonality, and facial expressions that she doesn't like what Nell draws in art class. To protect herself, Nell's unconscious builds a wall around her spontaneity, allowing no external expression of it. This protects Nell from the teacher's criticism but severely limits her as 30-year-old writer. Whenever external circumstances call for something creative and spontaneous, Nell's unconscious erects a wall and shuts her down.

We will now examine the eight categories of Internal/External Boundaries: Projection/Isolation, Mode, Causality, Polarity, Generalization, Threshold, Identity, and Time.

1. Projection/Isolation

I'm sure you've had the experience of meeting someone and taking an instant dislike to that person. What triggered your response? Over time, your initial judgment may or may not have been proven accurate.

> Peter was forced to spend time with Barbara because they worked together. Initially he disliked her, but as he got to know her, he actually began to appreciate her. It was a mystery to him why he had had such a negative reaction to her at first until he became aware that her tone of voice unconsciously reminded him of a first-grade teacher who had been very mean to him. He had lost his internal/external boundaries with Barbara: the memory of his teacher merged with his colleague, Barbara. Her tone of voice

reminded him of the painful experiences that triggered those original emotions back in first grade. He lost his perspective: his colleague was not his first-grade teacher, even though it felt as if she were. As soon as he became aware of the similarity of their voices, he no longer experienced the old response. With awareness and boundaries, he could appreciate Barbara for who she was, separate from the memory of his teacher.

When we go to the movies or read a good novel, we want, at least momentarily, to lose our boundaries. You're sitting in a movie theater with your feet on the sticky ground and your back against the chair, watching a large flat screen. Yet your heart begins to beat faster, your breath catches in your throat, and you may even gasp and grab the person's arm next to you as you hear the sound of the killer's footsteps and breathing as he walks down the dark hallway slowly and deliberately toward the closet where the heroine is hiding. You may be watching images of lovers parting forever, because of circumstances beyond their control, and you begin to cry. How is this possible? You're sitting safely in a movie theater, watching pictures projected on a two-dimensional screen.

You've lost the distinction between yourself, where and who you are, and the pictures on the screen. You've leaped over that distinction and entered a fantasy world, making that world your reality. The lines between *you* and *not you* have evaporated. Why else go to the movies or read a good story but to enter another world or become someone else? How many times have you laughed out loud or cried out in pain at something you're reading? Isn't that the mark of a good book?

These are examples of Projection in the category of Projection/ Isolation, when you blur the distinction between a situation or person in the external world and your inner thoughts, memories, or emotions. You merge the two. When you distort your boundaries in this way there is always a loss of boundaries.

On the other hand, when walls are created between your internal and external worlds, isolation results.

Consider the policeman whose work at times involves the terrible images and sounds of the cruelty of one human being toward another. He learns to protect himself from this pain and suffering by building walls. This is useful and beneficial, enabling him to do his job and function. Except when it becomes a habit and the walls are there all the time; with his colleagues, his family, the victims. He becomes a cold, detached, cut-off human being who loses the ability to connect, to feel empathy, and to be vulnerable.

My son is a volunteer EMT (emergency medical technician) and he really cares about the people he helps. When assisting with serious accidents, he sometimes has trouble keeping his boundaries and gets overly emotionally involved. He's told me about some EMTs who have been working for a long time and have become detached from the patients, treating them like objects. They have learned to build walls to protect themselves, but now they do so with every patient and every situation. All they can offer is a mechanical type of assistance and no human comfort.

A person who has been severely traumatized as a child because of abuse, neglect, or alarming manipulation will build walls in order to survive. Listen to soldiers who were prisoners of war describe what they did to survive. They imagined being somewhere else; built imaginary shields around themselves; thought of their tormentors as small and far away; withdrew deep inside themselves so nobody could get to them, thought of themselves as split off from their bodies (the real self separate from the body shell). This is how you build walls and it is a good example of when walls can help. However, when the walls become permanent, when there's no choice, you become trapped inside the walls of your own prison, and connection becomes frighteningly difficult or impossible.

2. Mode

Have you ever felt guilty when you've found yourself attracted to someone who is not your significant other? Here you are in a committed relationship, yet you're having fantasies about someone else. You might feel so guilty that you "confess" to your lover and all hell breaks loose. Wait a minute! Have you done anything? Actually acted on your thoughts and feelings? If not, what are you guilty about? You feel guilty because you've lost your boundaries between thinking and doing.

The second category of Internal/External Boundaries is Mode. People interact with the world in three different Modes: through *thinking* (remembering or imagining images, words, sounds, tastes, and smells); through *feeling* emotions; and through *doing* or acting in the external world (speaking, gesturing, opening a box, driving a car, climbing stairs, and so on). These three Modes are separate and distinct from each other. However, with boundaries in place, they strongly affect each other. Without boundaries, they merge. Thinking becomes the same as doing; doing the same as feeling. This results in confusion. When there are walls, each Mode is isolated from the other, and the Modes have no impact or influence on each other.

> Mark is a young and talented supervisor; he appreciates and respects the team of social workers for whom he's responsible. Their well-being and success is important to him, and he's very aware of the excellent work they do. Over time, his team has become demoralized, and Mark doesn't understand why. Finally, one of them confronts him, saying, "We work hard and do good work, but you never say anything about that. We don't feel appreciated at all!" Mark is dumbfounded, because he does appreciate them. However, for him, thinking is the same as speaking out loud. He has told his team that he appreciates them, over and over again, but only inside his mind.

A 10-year-old girl has a fantasy of beating up her brother and dropping him out of the second-story window. He's been really mean to her lately; not letting her go with him and his friends to the park. He's always telling her, "Get lost, squirt!" She tells her mother what she wants to do to him. Her mother is horrified, lectures her, tells her father, and they ground her for a month. They keep telling her what a bad girl she is to have such evil thoughts. Her parents responded to her fantasies as though she had acted on them. They scolded her instead of telling her that they understood she was hurt and angry at her brother, explaining that he was getting older and wanted his own space. They neglected to explain that while thoughts and feelings are one thing, no matter how angry she felt, she must never actually *do* anything physically violent to her brother. Because her parents lost the boundaries between their daughter's thoughts and her behavior, they may have damaged her self-esteem—and missed an opportunity to help her understand the difference between thinking and doing.

> Albert has lots of ideas about what he wants to do with his life. One week, he's going to go to bartending school so he can get a job and support himself while he goes back to university to get his teaching degree. The following week, he's going to start his own limousine service, ferrying people back and forth to the city, a hundred miles away. Another week, he is going to move to Alaska and open a restaurant. And so it goes! He's constantly thinking of how he's going to fix up his house, help his parents, or get a better job, but he never does anything to make these ideas happen. There is such a wall between his thoughts and taking action that there's no connection between the two, no essential realization that thought sets the goal, emotion motivates, and action makes it happen.

3. Causality

The third category is Causality. There is a normal, logical causality between certain actions. A ringing telephone generally prompts you to pick it up. Of course, you could choose not to, but there is a logical connection between these two events. Someone you meet puts out his hand in that universal gesture of shaking hands, and you respond by putting out your hand. A sudden loud noise makes you jump. These are situations when you can assume a normal causality exists. However, when walls are present or boundaries are lacking, there can be a severe distortion of reality. For instance, what is your response when you've had mean thoughts about someone and then something terrible happens to him? Do you feel somehow responsible? Children can be deeply traumatized when they get angry at a parent and say things like "I hate you" or "I wish you were dead," and then that parent gets hurt or dies in an accident. The child blames herself because she thought it and said it, and then it happened. She has no boundaries between her thoughts, feelings, and words and the external event of the accident. It's as though she made it happen. The lack of boundaries between her inner experience and the external event of the accident creates a false causality.

Imagine you're in a situation that is very embarrassing and you wish with all your heart that you weren't there, that you could just disappear. What do you do? You close your eyes, just like the child who covers his eyes and says, "Now you can't see me!" Because of a loss of boundaries, you assume a causality that doesn't exist. When you close your eyes and can't see anything, you "become invisible"—the outside world cannot see you!

Consider the person who blames himself when bad things happen. He accepts a ride with you to the train station and your car breaks down. He may say, "I'm sorry, whenever I'm around things seem to go wrong." Or the neighbor who comes to your son's outdoor wedding and it begins to rain heavily. She says, "I always seem to bring bad luck!" Have you ever noticed that some people keep saying "I'm sorry" whenever difficult or uncomfortable things happen around them, even though they have nothing to do with them? This is known as "magical thinking," and it promotes "center of the universe" syndrome. Babies and young children *are* the center of their universe, and that is as it should be. However, by the time they are 18, they should be realizing that the world does *not* revolve around them. Appropriate boundaries between cause and effect in your life help you to accept this.

On the other hand, walls between two related events prevent connection between behavior and the effects of behavior. We learn only when we experience consequences, and boundaries allow us to make the connection between our behavior and consequences.

A young man is feeling lonely and despondent. A good friend in a far-away state invites him to visit, and he jumps at the chance to see his friend and escape his present circumstances. He has such a good time that he stays longer than he had planned, longer than the vacation time he had been granted at his job. When he returns, he is fired. He complains that his boss is insensitive and wanted to fire him anyway because of office politics. He doesn't take responsibility for his actions, and he certainly is not going to learn anything useful from this experience. With walls preventing any sense of cause and effect, he maintains total separation between his actions—taking more vacation time than that agreed upon and, as a result, getting fired.

Walls like this support "the blame game." You blame someone or something else for your misfortune, because you're keeping your behavior and the results of your behavior separate.

4. Polarity

In the first three categories, Projection/Isolation, Mode, and Causality, there can be walls, loss of boundaries or, of course, boundaries. In the fourth category, Polarity, there are only walls. Polarities occur when there is a dichotomy between two absolutes: all or nothing, good or bad, right or wrong—indeed any either/or situation. For example, "I can be rich or spiritual," "I can think or feel," "I'm attractive or ugly, a genius or stupid." Polarities are the two ends of a black-and-white spectrum with no gray options in-between. In order for a Polarity to exist, there must be a solid wall between the two ends of this spectrum.

> Jim is a public speaker who is very successful; however, when he has to speak on a new topic or to a type of group he's never before addressed, he panics. He's either completely confident or he's totally incompetent. Confident for him means never having doubts or making mistakes, so when he does question himself or make a mistake, he immediately falls into the despair of "I can't do anything." The separation between confident and incompetent is complete; there's no connection between mistakes and learning or improving. With boundaries, Jim will learn that true confidence is not about never making mistakes: it's about being able to make a mistake and being confident that you can deal with it and learn.

Another example of Polarity is the mother who must be *completely* patient with her children at *all* times, no matter how stressful the circumstances are. If she loses it and snaps at one of them, she becomes, in her mind, a "bad mother." She has no connection between her inner concept of patience and her external reality.

Some of you may be plagued with the belief that you can think *or* feel, but it is impossible to do both at the same time. It is as though a wall cuts across your neck, separating your head from the rest of your body. Functional thinking *must* include feelings. Imagine how limited your thinking would be if it were not informed by your feelings. Or course, we make the distinction between thinking and feeling but not to the exclusion of one or the other.

Those of you for whom knowledge is safety or sanity may be frightened of your emotions; you attempt to detach from them, or allow yourself to experience them only when you're alone. When the walls do come down, you may bounce to a state without boundaries and become overwhelmed with your emotions with little access to your ability to think. Then you're caught in a dichotomy and self-fulfilling prophesy: *I can think or feel.*

> Gertrude is an accomplished architect who has learned how important precise, clear thinking is in her profession. She thinks very well and never lets those pesky feelings intrude in her work. She is always surprised when her clients don't seem to appreciate her—even when the home she produces for them is spectacular! Her people skills leave much to be desired. Because she is cut off from her feelings when interacting with her clients, she gives the impression of being cold and aloof. If she ever does let feelings into her work, she loses all boundaries and is completely inappropriate. On the other hand, in her personal life, she suffers. She continually chooses men who are cads, users, mean-spirited, or unavailable. She "goes with her feelings" totally in her love relationships and never uses her head. If she starts to think, she cuts off her feelings and becomes detached and gets nothing that she wants. She is in a loop that keeps proving itself over and over: "I can think or feel."

Consider the example of a single father who both loves his children and is ambitious to succeed as a lawyer. He believes that in order to be successful, he has to give two hundred percent of himself to his job. He also believes that in order to take proper care of his teenage children and keep them safe, he must be there for them all the time. He may turn down a high-powered job and feel diminished and discontented, or he might take the job and then feel guilty and constantly worried that something horrible is going to happen to his kids! The plague of either/or. He can either be a successful lawyer or a good father. In this case, the wall is between his ambition and his children.

With boundaries, you can transform the *either/or* in your life into *and!*

5. Generalization

The fifth category, Generalization, can support and expand learning when there are boundaries, but without boundaries, it becomes extremely limiting. A generalization identifies the common thread and the relationship between or among two or more experiences. When you have several positive experiences in a certain city, you might generalize that it is a good, fun city. You win the first couple of times that you play chess, and you decide you're good at the game. You understand what doors are because you can generalize to the overall purpose of doors, even when you encounter a type of door you've never seen before. When you lose boundaries, you lose the awareness that several experiences are separate from the whole and do not represent the whole experience. Another way to explain what happens when you lose boundaries in a generalization is that "a part equals the whole."

Have you ever had a "bad hair"day? Your hair is too curly, or flat, or straight, or whatever. It is not doing what it's supposed to do, and you feel terrible. All of a sudden you're unattractive, stupid, and incompetent. It's as though someone pulled the plug and your confidence and self-esteem leaks away. You've become your hair! The fact is that your hair is only a part of you; you still have your eyes, your body, your movement, your mind, and your compassion—all of you, your total being. But at that moment you've lost your awareness of the total "you" and become your hair.

If you've ever spent time around teenagers, you know how devastating a large pimple on the forehead or chin can be. A young boy totally loses his sense of self-worth and becomes a "walking pimple." He's devastated. He becomes self-conscious and convinced he's ugly and no one will talk to him or like him. This is another example of how "a part equals the whole." The distinction between a part of the person and the whole person is lost; the totality of a person is merged into her hair or his pimple.

Another example of generalization might occur when you receive feedback about your work. Your boss is pleased with most of your performance in the job, except for one area which he thinks you're neglecting; he wants you to clarify your goals and follow through more. With boundaries, you would understand that this is only a part of your performance, and his reaction to your work overall is positive. This is simply an opportunity to improve. If you fall into the trap of "a part equals the whole," you'll only hear and take in the part that he doesn't like and generalize that to your entire performance. You'll feel as though your boss thinks you've done a terrible job, that he hates your work, and is about to fire you! In the category of Generalization, only loss of boundaries applies.

6. Threshold

Do you know when enough is enough? When you have eaten enough? When you have enough money or success? When you're good enough? Handsome enough? Sexy enough? If you don't know when enough is enough, it means you have an issue in the sixth category of Internal/External Boundaries, Threshold. Threshold is about the values that you strive to achieve or avoid. It is the edge where you either jump or hold on, the doorway that marks the point of entering or leaving. It is the point or value above which something is true (and will happen) and below which it is not (and will not happen). "Leaving the old, both worlds at once they view, that stand upon the threshold of the new," as the English poet Edmund Waller (1606–1687) wrote *On Divine Poems*.

To know when enough of anything is enough means having awareness of your threshold: achieving your limit or falling short of it signals that either you can stop or must continue. In order to know when to stop eating, you must be aware of the separate sensations of hunger and being full and their relationship to each other. Have you ever eaten an entire quart of ice cream or a pound of candy by yourself? It's as though you lose the distinction between you and what you're eating—you become the ice cream!

> Pamela describes her experience with brownies. There is a wonderful bakery between her office and the station where she takes a train to get home. She loves brownies, and she can never eat just one.

This bakery makes the best brownies in the city! The staff put trays of these gorgeous, thick, brown, glistening squares in the window, and in warm weather, the smell drifts out into the street. Since she knows she can't resist these delicious brownies, she usually walks two blocks out of her way to get to the train station just so she won't have to pass by the bakery. One evening, she's late getting out of work, and she has an important date at home, so she decides to take the shorter albeit more dangerous route. She remembers seeing the brownies in the window, smelling that incredible smell, and the next thing she's conscious of is being a block away from the bakery, holding an empty bakery bag and licking sticky brown crumbs off her fingers. She feels that the brownies had called to her and literally taken over her—she has no memory of going into the store, buying the brownies, and walking a block while devouring them, until she "woke up" holding an empty bag!

Perhaps you think this story is a bit exaggerated. Is it? How many bags of potato chips or M&Ms have you finished before you even realized it? Pamela lost her boundaries between the external reality of smelling and tasting the brownies and her internal, physiological response. She was no longer aware of her internal sensations of fullness, and without that, it was impossible to know when enough was enough!

Consider success. Do you have such a rigid and unchanging idea of what success is that there's a lack of connection between your concept of success and your actual experience of it? If you do, it could be because there's a wall between your idea and your experience.

Take George, a man who grew up in a large, middle-class, struggling family that had trouble paying the monthly bills. There was never enough money to cover everything. His father was an inventor who never created the better mousetrap. Throughout his entire childhood he heard his mother talk about neighbors and friends who were "successful," unlike his father who never really made it. Success was defined as security: a guaranteed salary, pension, and retirement. The pinnacle of success was being in the civil service because your future was secure; you couldn't get fired. When he became an adult, George went to work in a large accounting firm. There were great benefits, a good pension plan that was guaranteed, and a safe retirement that he could look forward to—but George didn't feel successful.

He wasn't happy. He volunteered two nights a week to work with disadvantaged kids, and there, he felt that his life had some meaning. He dreaded going to work every morning and sitting alone in his cubicle, crunching numbers. He was successful! Miserable but successful. He had such solid walls around his definition of success that he allowed no input, no experience from the external world, into his belief about success. The fact that he was happier and more fulfilled working with kids had no impact upon him and was not allowed to change his idea of success. It was as though his experiential definition of success was inside a house with doors and windows that didn't open, never allowing the sunshine and fresh air from outside to come inside and shape the internal environment.

If there are walls between your inner definition of a value and your actual experience of it in the world, and if your definition doesn't include your emotional responses, then it's impossible to know when you're achieving your value rather than the *idea* of that value as passed on to you by family or society. When walls are present, you don't know when you're smart enough, pretty enough, successful enough, or when enough is enough for you!

7. Identity

Have you ever wondered why some people have so much trouble with retirement? They become depressed, despondent, restless, dissatisfied, bitter, and resentful, even when they have no financial worries. You wonder why they can't relax and do all the things they never had time to do when they were bringing up the children and working hard to secure this moment!

These are people whose identity is fused with what they do: their job, their role in the family, their possessions, or even a particular behavior. The belief "I am what I do" or "I am what I have" merges the external doing or external possessions with the inner totality of the person. The seventh category is Identity. It is important to consider Identity when your essential beingness is reduced to a role, job, behavior, possession, or status.

Of course, for the man who built his company from scratch, turned it into a multimillion-dollar enterprise that employed hundreds and contributed to the larger community, his job was very important and significant. But did he lose his boundaries and become consumed, becoming almost literally his company? For that man, retirement will be a nightmare. He has no other identity, so what will fill that empty hole when he gives up his job?

Many artists, writers, and musicians never "retire" but work until they drop. For them this path is probably best because they want no other identity; but some artists know that they are not their art, that their entire life is a work of art. The art and beauty of the mundane details of life gives true joy and contentment. This happens only when you are both connected and separate from those details, your work, your role in the family, your hobbies, or your avocation.

The "I am what I do" type of loss of boundaries can limit you not only in your job but in the things you do for pleasure. I live with and show Irish Wolfhounds. Usually I can enjoy showing them whether I win or lose. Of course, I'm very happy when I win, but if sometimes when I lose I start getting depressed and feel bad about myself and my dog, I know I'm losing my boundaries. My sense of *self* is getting mixed up with showing and winning instead of enjoying the sport and learning more about my dog and myself.

> Julie had been training for the New York marathon for years. She had become obsessed with running and finishing this marathon. Not winning, just finishing! This was certainly a worthy goal, but when Julie failed to finish the race, she became despondent and actually felt like she was a total failure. She began to believe that she would never finish anything and would fail at everything in her life.

A mother who makes no distinction between who she is and her role as a mother will feel that she's a "nothing" when her children grow up and leave home to create their separate lives. She has accomplished one of the most fundamental responsibilities of parenthood: to nurture and guide her children toward self-dependence in the world and create their own lives. However, she still feels terrible about herself because she has no sense of identity separate from her role as mother.

The totality of who you are is much more than your job, your profession, your art, your passion, your memories, your behavior, your role as mother, father, husband, lover, son, daughter, friend, caregiver, or warrior. This is the seventh category of Internal/External Boundaries, and only loss of boundaries applies.

8. Time

The eighth category of this level of boundaries is Time. This category is about how you experience yourself and the external world in relation to the past, present, and future.

Do you remember when you were a teenager and, although you had an important test the next day, you went to a really great party with your friends the night before? Instant gratification is possible only when you wall off the present from any future consequences and become enmeshed in your feelings of the moment. In this case, your *now* rules your life, and what you're feeling now is the only reality no matter how it might affect your future.

One of the most basic ways that you learn about yourself and motivate yourself is through consequences. When there's a wall between your present and your future, there's no connection to consequences, so it's as though they don't exist. (There can be a certain overlap between the categories of Causality and Time in terms of consequences.)

When you're attracted to someone and connected to the future, you take into consideration the consequences of acting on your feelings and make informed decisions. When the future is walled off and consequences don't exist, your actions could endanger your health or your relationship. Delayed gratification depends upon boundaries. One of the reasons it is so hard for many teenagers to motivate themselves or control their impulses is because there's a wall between the present and future. Consequences are not real to them—they may know there's a future, but there's no emotional connection.

The tendency to bounce from one extreme (walls) to the other extreme (no boundaries) causes the present to merge with the future. Loss of boundaries between the present and future extends the present into an endless infinity; the present and future become the same. It's great when you're enjoying yourself and happy, but what happens when you're depressed? This is one of the reasons that teenagers become suicidal. Something bad happens to them, such as not getting into the college of their choice, their parents divorce, or they lose their girlfriend or boyfriend. The normal disappointment, fear, or sadness gets intensified and they believe that they're going to feel this way forever. The future is the same as the present; nothing will ever change. The feeling that the future is going to be just like the present is one of the necessary elements of depression, and since teenagers are just beginning to stabilize their boundaries, this feeling can hit them hard.

Even when you're happy, having no boundaries between the present and future can seem great but actually has a downside. If the present is endless, how are you going to plan ahead and organize yourself? You might enjoy yourself for a while, but pretty soon, reality is going to catch up with you! You'll keep finding something pleasurable to distract yourself from organizing your life as you go in circles until you crash. There are times when you want to experience this kind of boundary loss to intensify and prolong certain states of being, but the key is being able to choose to do it with full awareness.

In order to learn from your mistakes and failures, you must experience the future as different from your present and your past. Your concept of the future that you get from the outside is connected to your inner experience. You're not walled off from limitless possibilities of the future, you understand that nothing lasts forever, and you are connected to your ability to learn, change, and do things differently because there's another chance at another time: the future. Being walled off into your present experience condemns you to what you are and know only now—nothing more.

Putting up walls between the present and past will protect you from the pain and trauma of the past, but if you allow it to become a habit, you'll lose valuable resources contained in that time. Even more importantly, you'll cut yourself off from an essential part of yourself. Dr. Milton H. Erickson, psychiatrist and one of the world's leading practitioners of medical hypnosis and hypnotherapy (1902–1980) maintained that "every experience, no matter how painful, is a potential resource."

> Norma was a successful executive who was attractive and smart, yet she suffered from persistent self-doubt. She couldn't seem to build a solid foundation of confidence. One day when we were working together, I asked her to create a road representing her past, with all her experiences lining each side. She complained that she couldn't see most of them because the road was so dark. I told her to turn on the lights, and after a moment her face lit up, her eyes got bigger, her voice was quick and loud as she exclaimed, "I'd forgotten all those things. I can't believe it!" Magically turning on a metaphoric light dissolved the walls that she had put around her past and revealed numerous memories that were positive and supportive. Her mind had shut the door on the past, on the positive as well as on the painful memories. She realized for the first time that she had had successes and accomplishments even when she was a child. This transformation of walls into boundaries in her past helped her build a foundation of self-confidence and a sense of worthiness.

One of the difficulties about emotions is the lack of boundaries between the present and the past. Your friend does something stupid or mean to you, and you get angry. The anger is justified, but in a matter of seconds, it has escalated into fury. This is not justified! What happened? You lost your boundaries between your present anger and past angers. Perhaps your friend unknowingly triggered similar feelings from the past, and they merged with the present emotion. Now imagine that your teenage son is an hour late coming home one night. You're understandably worried, but your worry quickly turns into panic. In both of these examples, a present emotion that was appropriate to the situation merged inappropriately with past memories of the same emotion, and transformed both situations into an unnecessary crisis. When contained by boundaries to the present circumstances, most emotions, while uncomfortable, usually can be dealt with by the person experiencing them and the person receiving them. It's the loss of boundaries with past emotions—the merging of past and present—that creates overwhelming emotions and an out-of-control situation.

When boundaries are lost, you can be constantly reliving the past. Once upon a time, you were betrayed by your lover. It's now years later, and you have a new lover. You're happy in this relationship, except that whenever she doesn't come home when she said that she would, and you can't reach her, you get suspicious that she's out betraying you with someone else. You get very paranoid, and by the time you reach her, you're accusing her of all sorts of horrible things. And she just got stuck in traffic, went to see her mother, or went out for a bite to eat with friends! Without boundaries, you can't put past experiences where they belong: in the past. They keep coming back into the present and contaminating your experience.

Inappropriate loss of boundaries or walls will distort your reality and severely limit you. Having Internal/External Boundaries enables you to separate and connect to your inner and outer worlds, allowing you to live with more choice and relate to others more successfully.

While having boundaries in each of these eight categories supports healthy and satisfying functioning in the world, and promotes your personal evolution, it is sometimes beneficial or pleasurable to choose to lose your boundaries or create walls. The advantages and disadvantages depend on knowing that you can choose to use the skills of "doing" boundaries or not. This level of Internal/External Boundaries you create is the essence of being separate and connected.

Once upon a time a son was born to the great racehorse Man o' War. His name was Sea Biscuit and he held the hopes and dreams of many that he would be as great or greater than his sire. For this reason he was given special care and attention. Nothing was too good for Sea Biscuit. He had the finest stall, most carefully monitored exercise, the best food and veterinary care.

Everything was carefully planned and carried out. When he became a yearling, his owners put him in his own special paddock. It was larger than any other horse's paddock and had a beautiful white fence around it. His caretakers were very excited on the day Sea Biscuit was to go into his new paddock. They were dismayed when the first thing he did was to go up to that beautiful fence and kick at it over and over again.

They all looked at each other and said, "Sea Biscuit must want more space." And so they built him a larger paddock. When he was put into that one he went over to that fence and kicked at it—repeatedly. They told each other, "Guess Sea Biscuit needs an even bigger paddock." When they put him into an even bigger paddock he did the same thing—kicked and kicked at the fence. Finally they built him a paddock so large that from the center of it you couldn't even see the fences. "Surely now, Sea Biscuit will be happy!" However, once he was in his huge paddock Sea Biscuit stood in the middle of it, dropped his head and was very depressed. Everyone was worried and confused. He wasn't eating very much or playing or running—he just stood there with his head hanging. No one knew what to do. One day a group of trainers from another part of the country was visiting the horse farm and among them was a very old and very wise trainer. Sea Biscuit's caretakers and trainers were desperate so they sought out this wise trainer and told him their tale of woe about Sea Biscuit and his paddock. The old wise trainer listened and watched Sea Biscuit until they finished. He smiled and told them he understood the problem and knew what had to be done. "Even though Sea Biscuit kicked at the fence in that first paddock you put him in, he needs those fences. He doesn't know that yet, but now in this huge paddock where he can't even see the boundaries of his space he is frightened and depressed. Put him back in that first paddock and let him kick for a while—he'll stop eventually and he'll feel safe again. Remember, horses need their fences."

Chapter III

Self/Other Boundaries

Within the larger category of "not me," there is another category of those "special" significant others. The foundation of successful relationships is human boundaries. This chapter explores the affect boundaries, no boundaries, or walls have on the relationships with the most important people in our lives. Intuition and assumptions are discussed within the frame of boundaries and the role they play in relationships.

Although boundaries in general always have to do with *me* and *not me* (that is, your internal and external worlds), within your external world there are more specific distinctions that are worthy of their own labels. These are Self/Other Boundaries (Other meaning "significant others") and Contextual Boundaries (defining different types of situation).

Self/Other Boundaries are the distinctions between you and the most important people in your life: your mate, partner, family, children, close friends, colleagues, mentors, and teachers. These are your "significant others." The nature of a significant relationship supports a deep, close connection that often blurs the distinction between you and the other. When there's hurt and pain, your first impulse is to build a wall to protect yourself, and sometimes this wall becomes habitual. It can be difficult to penetrate or let go of.

Tammy and Noelle have been best friends since they were 10 years old. Now they're 19, going to the same college, and both working on the same student newspaper as assistants, which is a fancy word for gofers. Both girls want to be reporters and write editorials. Tammy begins to notice that Noelle is acting strangely—she's hanging out a lot with the editor, a senior they both thought was a nerd, disappearing at times and then acting as though she hadn't. Finally, Tammy discovers that Noelle has been following up tips on stories by herself and is dating the editor without telling her. Tammy feels hurt and betrayed, especially when Noelle gets promoted to junior reporter and now will hardly give her the time of day. Tammy puts up a wall to protect herself. Two years later, she finds it difficult to make friends or to let herself get close to anyone. The wall between herself and her ex-friend generalized to all friends and became solid. A year after the newspaper incident, Noelle tried to apologize and renew their friendship, but Tammy wouldn't even consider it.

What mother or father does not feel pain when her or his daughter has been hurt in a relationship? But is this you empathizing with your daughter's pain, or do you take on her pain as though it were your own? For example, say that your teenage daughter's boyfriend dumps her for someone else, and she's very hurt. There you are, wandering around your house with this god-awful pain in the middle of your chest. Even though you know in your head it's not *you* who's been dumped, it feels like you have. You have lost your boundaries and are merging with your daughter and her pain.

Say that my son is angry because a teacher is being condescending to him, and he is threatening to punch the teacher. I get angry and begin to yell at my son for thinking about doing something that will endanger his entire school career and could negatively impact the rest of his life. I'm absorbing his anger and feeling it as though it were mine, acting as if I have to be angry because he's angry! Of course, when he feels this coming from me, it intensifies his feelings, he responds to *me* with anger, and the interaction escalates into a fight, making any meaningful communication impossible. Not only have I lost my boundaries between his feelings and mine, I have lost the opportunity to help him recognize the future consequences of his actions. I am not making any distinction (no boundaries) between his thoughts and his actions. I respond as though he had acted on his thoughts and feelings rather than simply voicing them.

Boundaries between parents and children are a huge challenge. Children don't have flexible and dependable boundaries, and they're not supposed to. Children do not have the psychological developmental patterns necessary to support consistent and stable boundaries. These are patterns that develop over time through their adolescence, teenage years, and early twenties (see Chapter 4).

The bonding or merging of newborns with their parents forms the basis of the ability to empathize and identify with others' feelings. Without this ability, the veneer of civilization would shatter. Laws and punishment are not enough to maintain civility; it is the fact that you can feel for another's pain, fear, despair, and can identify with these emotions that keeps you human.

Self/Other Boundaries begin to develop around 4 to 5 months of age and remain unstable and inconsistent until you reach your twenties. Babies and parents make few distinctions between each other, as is appropriate. As your child grows, you both begin to make more distinctions. She begins the slow process of individuation, or noticing differences between herself and her father and mother. She starts to realize that she is not her parents, and they are not her. It's not okay to bite mommy because that hurts her. It's not okay to tear up daddy's books because they are important to him.

Over time, your child becomes her own separate person with her own emotions, thoughts, values, and beliefs, and both parents and child have to recognize and honor this. However, because both are used to having few boundaries, this process is not easy or smooth! For both, merging is more familiar. For the growing adolescent, this can feel smothering, and she rebels and puts up walls to protect and separate herself from all the feelings and confusion. You as the parent must respond with boundaries, being separate and connected. This process can become so painful that sometimes you just want to sever the emotional connection. If you do so, you're both behind walls, and from this position it is almost impossible to communicate. As parents, you've had more experience creating boundaries, and you've developed the psychological patterns necessary to support boundaries, so it is primarily your responsibility to maintain your boundaries with your children while they flip-flop between walls and no boundaries. Eventually, as they develop the necessary patterns, they will learn how to have boundaries with you and life will be easier.

My daughter and I have always been very close, very tuned in to each other's feelings. As a very little girl, she was aware of what was important to me and honored that. I like to think that I was reasonable in my expectations of her and trusted her. It wasn't that she constantly tried to please me; she stood up to me, and I respected that, but she was very connected to me emotionally and was thus able to read my emotions and respond to them. During her late teenage years, she really separated from me. She put up walls and isolated herself from me emotionally. We were able to talk about it, and I understood that because of the almost psychic connection between us, she needed to detach from me in order to have the space to discover who she was, separate from me, what her emotions and values were separate from mine. It was very painful for both of us. Sometimes I'd get scared that we would never really connect again, but we did. After a few years, during which time we continued to talk and interact, we were once again emotionally connected and close. But it's different now. We're connecting as two separate, adult individuals, and there's a very special joy in this new connection. Do I miss the old connection? I'd be lying if I said no. I also know that in any case the old way could not, would not continue under any circumstances, and I can now mostly rejoice in this very special mother/daughter relationship.

Consider your relationship with your lover, husband, wife, or partner. Do you pride yourself on knowing what he feels and what he thinks even before he tells you? This happens in any intimate relationship. You become so familiar with each other's moods that, even without being conscious of it, you see and hear small indications that you've come to recognize as signs of irritability, anxiety, excitement, indifference, boredom, happiness, or other moods or states of mind. This is inevitable when spending a lot of time with someone; after all, part of the definition of intimacy is familiarity. Herein lies the danger!

When interacting with the people with whom you have a close and deep relationship, you tend to assume that your intuition is the truth—always. No matter how close you are to someone, no matter how connected you are, you are two unique and different individuals. Many times you are going to be right about what they are feeling, but sometimes you are going to be wrong. If you assume you "know the other," what happens when you're wrong, when your assumption is inaccurate? It could provoke a funny misstep, or it could develop into a serious miscommunication that may lead to more dangerous misunderstandings.

> James and Jill have been lovers for many months, and they have found great passion, humor, and companionship with each other. They have begun to sense that they may be soul mates. One night after dinner, they are enjoying some music, good books, and a fire. Jill has put on weight recently and found some gray hairs; she is feeling a bit unattractive. James seems restless: he puts the book down, walks around the room, and picks the book up again. Jill approaches him and begins to rub his shoulders and back and kisses his neck. He gets up and stirs the fire. She tries to kiss him again, and he starts to straighten up the room. Now what is the reality of this situation? Is it, as Jill senses, that James is losing interest in her sexually? Or is it that James is the kind of person who needs to be active, and he isn't moving away from her because he is tired of Jill but because he gets antsy when doing nothing for too long? Because of the excitement of the initial courtship, this hadn't really come up before, but now that they are evolving into a solid, long-term relationship, this part of James is reemerging. If Jill continues to lose her boundaries and believes that James doesn't find her attractive any more, she could pout or become angry, needy, cold, and detached, any of which could escalate into a rift. James has also lost his boundaries by assuming that she ought to understand his need to be active without ever specifically telling her. Now he might tell her that he's got to leave to go do something and get annoyed with her when she feels hurt—and so this could escalate into a full-blown fight with hurtful words and accusations! They could have avoided this situation by maintaining their boundaries and telling each other what they were thinking and feeling.

You don't want boundaries when you are making love. You want to merge, and that is a good thing. What about the rest of your relationship? If you try to stay merged the rest of the time, you'll end up half a person and part of a symbiotic relationship. One of you will feel smothered, and the other will feel burdened. It is the flow between dependence and independence, between intimacy and individuality, that creates a functioning, evolving relationship. In the short run, it would be a lot easier if you could be one way or the other, dependent or independent (there's that dichotomy again). The challenge is in free choice and awareness: choosing to let go of all boundaries and merge and then choosing again to be your separate self and remain connected. Most symbiotic relationships don't work, because there are no longer two separate whole individuals choosing to interact. Without that separation and wholeness, there is too much buried resentment, frustration, and disappointment to support the positive evolution of two people. In any functioning relationship, there are three separate entities: two whole individuals and the relationship between these two. The awareness and knowledge of boundaries and how to "do" them helps keep these three entities alive and well. "A good marriage is that in which each appoints the other guardian of his solitude." (*Duino Elegies*, Rainer Maria Rilke, 1875–1926)

Intuition is a wonderful tool and a great gift that should be nurtured and developed. Being able to unconsciously put together and incorporate what you experience with your senses, your knowledge of the other, and the wisdom gained from all your past experiences allows you to create new insights and new ideas. Everyone has the capacity to be intuitive. Two things are necessary to develop your intuition: observation skills and trusting your unconscious. The more observant you are, the more raw material you acquire for your unconscious to process. Trusting your unconscious does not mean believing that anything your unconscious comes up with is the truth; it means trusting the process and remembering that this intuitive ability comes from your model of the world. What you do with your intuition is as important as having intuition. To assume that your idea, your insight, is the truth is not using this gift wisely. This is *mind reading*. You are assuming the truth of something about another individual without any concrete, external evidence. The key word here is *assume*. Honor your intuition by claiming ownership, and respect the other person by checking your assumption with them: "I may be wrong, but are you angry?" "I sense that you're not in the mood right now—is it me or something else?" "I have a hunch that you really don't want to go to that concert. Am I right or wrong?"

Mind reading is an example of losing boundaries between yourself and someone else. You are assuming that someone else's gesture, facial expression, posture, or tone of voice has the meaning that *you* have assigned to it. Intuition is the unconscious process that creates a new thought or conclusion. However, when you assume that an intuitive thought is "the" truth and impose it on another person, you've lost the distinction between your own reality and the other person's reality. Use the gift of intuition, but do not fall in love with your conclusions! Respect and honor the other person by remembering that you are two distinct individuals.

When you look at someone and you notice how he's different from you—he's shorter, fatter, older, younger, more talkative, or any number of different characteristics—you're establishing *separateness*, not *isolation*. Differences create distinctions that equal separateness. When you have trouble tolerating difference, it means that you're more comfortable with sameness or familiarity, a situation that can lead to having no boundaries. Perhaps you equate separation with isolation or alienation. When you think you know the other's thoughts and feel the other's emotions, you define that as connection. This is an illusion that actually, if it persists over time, has the opposite effect: as you lose more of your self, you're less able to recognize the true nature of the other. This boundary disturbance often manifests itself as horror or panic when your loved one gets angry with you or you get angry with her. You feel abandoned and rejected when her opinion differs from yours, or she wants to take up some hobby in which you have no interest. You experience any demonstration of difference as a threat to your relationship and sometimes to your very existence. The more you need sameness and familiarity, the less tolerant and flexible you become. You feel more needy and dependent, which fuels insecurity, anger, and resentment. The more that you need merging and enmeshment with no separation, the more you manifest a loss of boundaries. I maintain that you cannot have true connection *without* separation.

The flip side of this is the *need* to maintain separation. You experience becoming connected to someone as a threat to your individuality; you fear that you could lose yourself and disappear. You might feel that the only protection against this threat is to emphasize difference, separateness in the extreme, and put up rigid walls. Of course, doing so makes it very difficult for you to connect with others, except perhaps with those who also have walls, as you may feel a certain comfort in your mutual isolation. You certainly are going to find it next to impossible to empathize with others, because that means stepping into the other's shoes. This is very frightening for those who depend primarily on separation for their identity. You cannot empathize if you cannot recognize and identify with others' emotions, cannot recognize that you've had similar emotions and can acknowledge the validity of your own and others' emotions, and cannot share your emotions with them.

I love to look at, touch, and smell my gardens in the three seasons that are available to me. I'm not an expert, and I need help because of the arthritis that complains loudly when I bend, lift, or carry too much. I can't really call myself a "gardener," which is a mighty title, but I do love to play at gardening.

> One early spring day, after a particularly cold and endless winter, I was in the garden sitting on my "grasshopper," a little contraption on wheels that allows me to sit close to the ground and push myself from place to place. I was attacking those first weeds, loosening the dirt after the long freeze and preparing the garden for some new rose bushes. I was getting my hands and fingernails gloriously dirty. The sweet smell of freshly turned dirt, the promise of spring in the air, and the sounds of very busy birds filled me with contentment and peace. I was at one with Mother Nature. After an hour or so of this joyful work, Tom stopped by in his pick-up to check with me about when I wanted him to help me dig the holes for the roses and do the mulching. We began to chat, and he told me about an encounter he had had with a customer who was extremely rude and condescending to him. Tom was very agitated about this and described his feelings to me in great detail for the next ten minutes. I was quite sympathetic and thought Tom had every right to be upset. We settled on next week's schedule, and he left. I went back to my gardening, but I couldn't get back into the peaceful, joyous state that I had been in before Tom's visit. Actually, I was very agitated and unsettled. "What is the matter with me?" I kept thinking, "Everything is fine, just enjoy your gardening." But I couldn't. This went on for a few minutes until I realized what had happened, and I'm sure by now you too have an idea. I had joyfully

abandoned my boundaries and totally merged with the earth, sky, birds, worms, the feel and smell of nature before Tom came into my space. When he did, he was agitated and upset. Since I had set no boundaries, I was very open and vulnerable. And he was, after all, part of my gardening experience and so I unknowingly took on his feelings—his agitation. I didn't realize what had happened at first, but when I did, I was finally able to let go of his agitation (which was not mine in the first place) and after a few more minutes was able to get back into enjoying the dirt once again.

This story is an example of the *positive* loss of Internal/External Boundaries between me and nature and the *negative* loss of Self/Other Boundaries between me and Tom.

Once upon a time, there was a very talented baker who lived and worked in a small village. He was such a good baker that his bread was famous for a hundred miles around. Now everyone knows that bakers have many secrets, and he was no exception, but, of course, no one tried to discover what his secrets were. And sometimes on Sundays, the baker would bake cakes as well as bread.

One Sunday, this baker decided to bake a very special cake and he named it the Courageous Child's Cake. This cake was for the child who exhibited especially courageous behavior, like the little boy who agreed to walk his younger sister to school every morning without grumbling or the girl who helped the old woman who lived at the end of the village to carry her groceries home. Then there was the child who helped her friend swim across the river when he was frightened, and the boy who for the first time got an excellent grade in mathematics.

Thus the Courageous Child's Cake became a tradition in the village. Whenever their children behaved in a special way, the parents, with great ceremony, would buy this cake for him or her. Everyone noticed that after the children ate the cake, they became even more courageous. People all whispered about what secret ingredient the baker was putting in the Courageous Child's Cake, but no one seriously tried to find out what it was, and everyone took advantage of this very special tradition.

Then two parents got a strange idea: they bought the Courageous Child's Cake for their child even though he had not done anything especially courageous! People began to grumble that that was not how it should be done and complain that those parents were violating an important tradition. However, when people began to observe that, after eating the cake, this child actually behaved in especially wonderful ways, they all agreed that it was all right to give the children the Courageous Child's Cake even before they did something courageous. And now, not only is this village famous for a hundred miles around for its bread, it has become even more famous for the courage and specialness of its children. No one has yet discovered the baker's secret; perhaps you have some ideas!

Adapted from a story by Patrick Condamin

Chapter IV

Contextual Boundaries

How do we know how to behave or what to expect in different situations? Different values or standards apply, and we shift our behavior and expectations according to the environmental cues we're receiving. This chapter describes the five categories of Contextual Boundaries: Place, People, Activity, Time, and Gender.

When you were 4 or 5 years old, you probably began to realize that using certain words around Grandma and Grandpa was not okay even though you could say them at home with your parents and siblings. You were beginning to make another kind of distinction, one that helped you understand that different situations or contexts had different rules for appropriate behavior: "Certain language is okay at home but not at Grandma's." It is around age 4 to 5 that you begin to develop *Contextual Boundaries* that are likely to remain unsophisticated and inconsistent until your late teens or early twenties.

There are many different types of situations in the external world, and they require different behavior and expectations. When you go to a foreign country and encounter a very different culture, it's important to know the rules for polite and acceptable behavior. In some cultures, getting physically close to someone when conversing is considered rude and offensive; in others, it is considered a sign of interest in and appreciation of the other. When you know these rules, your experience will be much smoother. You will be treated better, and it will be easier for you to communicate your needs and to connect with the people and the place.

It is not just in foreign cultures where you must understand the different rules for appropriate behavior and expectations. In everyday life, this is *equally* important. The distinctions you make between various circumstances allow you to know what to expect from yourself, others, and the situation itself, as well as what behavior is appropriate. These Contextual Boundaries help you to make friends, succeed, create a positive impression, and avoid unnecessary sanction and disapproval. This level of boundaries includes five categories: *Place, People, Activity, Time,* and *Gender.*

1. *Place*

> As my youngest son got ready to go to kindergarten, I was concerned about how he would respond. Until then, he had gone to a small, family-oriented nursery school, but this was "real" school. In our home, my children and I use "colorful language." Never to denigrate others but more as an expressive tool! For a number of years, I had told Raven that there were some places, like Grandma's house or public places, where that kind of language was inappropriate. School was one of these places. I had met his kindergarten teacher, Mrs. White, and while she was a kind and gentle person, she was very proper! I knew that if Raven used some of his favorite "colorful" expressions, she would be shocked and probably think less of him. He was a sweet and charming little boy, if a bit strong willed, and I was worried that he might create a negative impression that wouldn't be a true reflection of his essential nature. So I kept my fingers crossed! One day after school, I stopped to talk to Mrs. White about Raven's first week, and she immediately told me what a charming, delightful little boy he was! Whew! I knew then that he had made the contextual boundary between home and school.

The first category of Contextual Boundaries is Place. It is an environmental cue that helps to define different situations. You make distinctions between different types of places such as school and home. Other examples of this category are office and nightclub, home and church, a neighbor's car and your own, the library and playground, the bank and the stables. In each case, the contextual boundary defines the place and the kind of behavior and expectations that are appropriate within it. This includes the kind of clothing to wear, the type of language to use, the degree of physical contact, expressiveness, freedom of movement, volume of voice, consideration of self and others—and just about all aspects of your behavior. You do not behave the same in a nightclub as you do in a church (or you don't as soon as you recognize the difference between these places). When you make a presentation before the board of directors of a bank and one before your local PTA, you even dress differently. A surgeon in a hospital cannot allow his feelings for his patient to interfere with his work, so he learns to detach himself from his emotions in order to use his skills to the best of his ability. Often this pattern becomes so habitual that he no longer makes the distinction emotionally between the hospital and his home. Without realizing it, he may become emotionally distant from his wife and children, which can cause all sorts of problems in his family life.

What if you walked into a library and didn't make the distinction between the library and a restaurant in terms of your behavior? After all, they're both public places! You'd make a very negative impression and annoy a lot of people if you spoke as loudly in the library as you do when dining out.

2. People

In the category of People, think of all the different types of people that you know: children and old people, teachers and friends, rabbis and priests, police and neighbors, bosses and colleagues. When you put excessively rigid boundaries or walls around a certain type of people, you limit yourself and your responses. Imagine that as a youngster you had very strict parents, teachers, and clergy around you and you developed a rigid idea of what people in authority were like. Your response became one of resentment and oversensitivity to any indication of authority. At 30, you might still respond this way to anyone in a position of authority. When you transform those walls into boundaries, you'll be able to connect to those individuals in authority positions and have some choice about your reactions rather than being trapped by knee-jerk responses.

The college professor who treats his students as though they are his friends has damaged his ability to teach and his students to learn. This loss of boundaries causes unnecessary pain and confusion when the professor has to give a low mark or negative feedback to a student who he considered a "friend." In this case, the familiarity of friendship interferes with the rigor of the learning process. It creates a sense of betrayal on the part of the students, and frustration and disappointment on the part of the professor, who may expect his students to understand his different roles even when he blurs the distinction.

3. *Activity*

The third category of Contextual Boundaries is Activity. The need for this boundary was obvious in the case of Betty, a senior executive of a medium-sized company, who recommended her friend, Pam, for a secretarial job at the company. Betty and Pam had children in the same school and often had something to eat together before or after PTA meetings or other school-related activities. A problem began to arise when Pam expected Betty to chat with her during office hours and got upset because Betty was not being "friendly." Pam did not have clear boundaries between working and socializing.

A classic example of activity boundaries shows up at the Christmas office party. Practically every office has one. An office party is fraught with traps. Is it a party or is it work? It labels itself as a party, but does that mean you can act the way you would at any party? Get a little drunk, make a pass at that good-looking woman who happens to be your boss, tell dirty jokes and laugh very loudly? Well, why not? It is a party! Except it's an *office* party. That means the context is *work*. You'd probably be better off if you defined that party as *work* and let the appropriate rules guide your behavior.

> Years ago my daughter decided to take one of my 24-hour day trainings. This was a challenge for both of us. We had always interacted within the context of mother and daughter, but now we would be interacting in a whole new context: teacher and student. Different behavior and expectations were called for! We agreed that once she entered the training room, she became a student, and I was the teacher. I put on my teacher's hat and treated her as I would any other student. My context was teaching, and she had expectations that were appropriate to have as a student: her context was learning. It worked out so well that people never knew she was my daughter until the end of the training when I could once again put on my proud mother's hat. An unforeseen benefit from

that experience was that it allowed us to see each other outside the context of mother and daughter. It is rare that you can truly experience your parent or child as who she is as a unique individual separate from your familial relationship.

Different activities call for different behavior and expectations. Working or playing a one-on-one sport such as tennis or a team sport like soccer, teaching or counseling, parenting or caretaking, consulting or supervising, managing or coaching all differ markedly. When you work and play with the same person, you expect very different things from him in these two activities. When working, he must be respectful, focused, and efficient, but when playing he can joke, touch you, and be silly. These types of distinctions present useful questions: what is the difference between managing and coaching? Or between consulting and supervising? The answers help you to better define what your behavior and your expectations should be.

I am a teacher and therapist, and while both activities have certain similarities, there are very significant differences. When I'm working with the same person in both activities, it is crucial that I am clear about these distinctions. What someone can legitimately expect from me as a therapist and what he can expect in a teaching situation are very different. In therapy, you speak about private, personal issues, and the client rightfully expects the therapist's undivided attention for the entire time spent together. In contrast, in a teaching situation, you cannot expect the prolonged undivided attention of the teacher, and the expectation of an in-depth exploration of a private matter is usually unrealistic and inappropriate. Becoming involved with a student in an outside context can be fraught with danger even when you maintain your boundaries.

> One of my students, Nora, was a judge, and we decided to create a divorce mediation center. However, as we explored this possibility, it soon became obvious that we had very different ideas about what mediation was and how a center should be structured. The project didn't work out. Unfortunately, she took it personally. She got quite upset with me and wasn't able to keep separate our relationship in the two different contexts: possible partners working together and the learning/teaching activities of the training. Within the latter context, she became defensive and confrontational when I gave

instructions for an exercise or explained a concept. I realized too late that my being able to maintain my boundaries didn't mean that she could maintain hers! For me, it was unfortunate that our business partnership didn't work out but that had nothing to do with our relationship as teacher and student. As I write this, I'm aware of how naive I was.

4. Time

Labels relating to time create specific contexts of their own: old, young, Saturday night, Christmas morning. This type of Contextual Boundary is very different from the Internal/External boundary of time, which relates to how you experience time itself—the very structure of past, present, and future. Contextual time boundaries have to do with more superficial labels.

Let us consider holidays. What makes a Thanksgiving family dinner different from the monthly family dinner? Why can't Christmas dinner be the simple, warm, and friendly time that Sunday dinner is? The holiday dinner has a special label, and the boundaries are usually very rigid so that the distinctions can become walls. Within those walls, there are absolute expectations: everybody must have a good time, be friendly and loving to each other, and be happy! On the other hand, at the regular Sunday dinner, people can be irritable, detached, or bored—and mood doesn't make for disaster or create a huge family problem. When holidays become rigidly defined, you have to fit inside that frame whether you like it or not, and when people don't fit, holidays make them miserable!

There was a time when you *had* to go out on Saturday night or else you were a failure—nobody liked you! Or New Year's Eve when you *had* to do something special and have a good time! Or else! You made these distinctions, but they were walled off from reality. There was no permeability, no impact from your experiences, and as a result, the rules for behavior and expectations became rigid and inflexible.

Labels relating to time help make important distinctions; however, are those distinctions boundaries or walls? Consider the labels of young, middle aged, and old. Are your definitions of these labels dynamic and changing according to the people, circumstances, and situations, or are they set in stone, immutable and immovable? Do you mourn your lost youth? Does society exalt the young and ignore or deny the old? Do you avoid labeling yourself as old because that means resignation and loss? Does middle-age conjure up images of the structured, safe, and boring life?

Boundaries that are permeable allow the constant flow of information to influence the meaning of the experience. Any of these labels—youth, middle age, and old age—are what you make of them. They are unique for each individual according to the events that shape their inner relationship with the world. When you decide what the meaning of a particular time distinction is and resist any information (from perception, cognition, sensation, or emotion) that could shift that meaning, you've put walls around your experiential definition and become trapped inside it. Boundaries allow your constantly changing relationship with time to keep evolving. Time never stops—it keeps changing, and you change with it.

Does this mean that it is better to have no labels regarding time? Let's look at what happens when you eliminate distinctions about time. Young, middle aged, and old cease to exist; you make no distinction between young and old. Without these distinctions, a 70-year-old woman may wear the same style of clothes and makeup she did when she was 20. That is not attractive and gives the impression of someone who hates what she is and is desperate to hold on to something that is long gone. That is sad, for each age has its own specialness and beauty. And that's not to say when you're 70 you have to wear dowdy clothes and old-lady shoes!

I knew a family who decided that holidays were artificial and stupid, so they treated them as though they didn't exist. No special picnic for the Fourth of July, no feast for Thanksgiving, and certainly no presents for Christmas or birthdays. Without experiencing those days as something special, the family lost the opportunity to celebrate and to exchange external manifestations of love and caring, and they became very somber and self-centered. Life has a way of engulfing you in the mundane and everyday responsibilities. Holidays shouldn't become rigid ideas of what should be but permeable labels that remind you to take a breath and to celebrate and share with family and friends.

5. *Gender*

The fifth category of Contextual Boundaries is Gender. You may be thinking, "That's rather obvious. Of course, there's a distinction between men and women!" But are you aware when you've got boundaries, no boundaries, or walls around those distinctions? Look at the way the rules and expectations about women's roles have changed in the last century. There was a time when women were considered property; they could not inherit or own a business. Despite these rigid ideas of appropriateness, some women broke the rules by subterfuge, by using a man's name or by having a man represent her (hence the phrase, "The power behind the throne").

Both men's and women's roles were rigidly defined: men were the breadwinners and protectors, women were the housekeepers and caretakers—and never the twain shall meet! Within those walls were fixed concepts of masculinity and femininity. Higher education for women was frowned upon because intelligent, educated women were not feminine. Real men didn't cry and certainly didn't get "emotional," except in anger! That's manly. Over the years there's been a gradual shift from walls to boundaries. Many factors have contributed to the awakening realization of the potential of men and women, but the fundamental shift in male/female roles has been from walls to boundaries.

Today, at least in Western cultures, the idea that women are property is absurd. There are women in every known profession. Women own every kind of business, including professional sports teams, and the laws of inheritance have nothing to do with gender. Men are nurses, women are doctors, men are ballet dancers, and women are fighter pilots and jockeys; the list is endless. I know several happy, functioning couples where the man stays home, runs the house, and cares for the children while the woman goes to work and financially supports the family.

Of course, there are still many examples of rigid concepts about what is appropriate for a man or a woman. A woman coaching a professional football team? Until recently, most of the publicly recognized great chefs of the world were men—women were cooks, men were chefs. As the walls between men and women have opened up, so that individual experience and potential determine the rules, there is sometimes a loss of boundaries. This can cause confusion and lack of structure in roles within a company or family. A role can be like a frame that holds and presents to the world the work of art within it. A role can be an opportunity for people to express who they are based not on others' beliefs but on their unique abilities and desires. Without roles, there's no structure, and this can make it harder to find yourself and work harmoniously with others. However, you must decide what role you want to embrace and how to shape it, giving yourself the freedom to change that role as circumstances change.

Ask yourself whether you're limiting yourself because of your own subtle assumptions based on your gender or belief about what's possible. If you want a flat, nondifferentiated playing field, are you stopping yourself from developing aspects of yourself that could be considered old-fashioned, like being a stay-at-home mother? It's important that we allow boundaries between men and women, not built on stereotypic ideas but on individual potential, sensitivity, and experience.

Different contexts call for different behaviors and expectations, and these different contexts are separated from one another by boundaries. When contexts are walled off from each other, there is little movement and connection between them. It's as though you put different situations in their own cubby holes and close them off. Only when you enter one do you contact the emotions, thoughts, or behavior particular to that one, with no connection to the other cubby holes. Whenever I talk about this idea, I'm reminded of the sea captain who had a wife and children in each seaport he visited. He was totally committed to each when he was with them, but when he left each port, he put that family back in their box and didn't consider them until the next time he was with them. As the saying goes, it was "out of sight, out of mind."

Cindy described a problem that she had at work. As an executive, she was able to stand up for herself and say no to her peers when she thought it appropriate, but when she was around her in-laws, she never seemed to be able to speak up for herself and take a stand on important issues. She had the ability to do so, but this ability was stuck in the box labeled "work" and was not available to her in the box called "in-laws."

The sea captain compartmentalized his life so well because he had built thick walls around each port he visited. Different stories but the same structure; walls around different contexts. One affecting external reality—the sea captain; the other affecting internal reality—Cindy's resources, her ability to stand up for herself.

When there is a lack of boundaries between different contexts, you can't know how you should behave or what to expect, and it's easy to act inappropriately or be disappointed because you have unrealistic expectations. Imagine trying to recreate the same garden you had in the Northeast when you move to Arizona. Of course you'll be disappointed and frustrated, because your expectations are not realistic. You've merged your expectations of two different geographic areas with different soil and climate.

A consultant I knew was a very powerful and successful motivational speaker. He developed exciting and energizing presentations for salespeople and sales managers. He was quite confident until he presented to a group where he fell flat! He soon realized his mistake. He forgot that a group of bankers is a very different "animal" than a group of salespeople!

You even use Contextual Boundaries to decide what clothes to wear; whether in business or in personal situations, you ask yourself what type of group you are meeting or socializing with. A young actress describes her experience moving from the environment of off-off Broadway, off-Broadway, and Broadway: when auditioning for off-off Broadway anything was OK! The more outrageous the better—flea market chic. Off-Broadway she could be outrageous but her clothes had to have class—downtown designer type styles. For Broadway she had to be tailored, very Saks Fifth Avenue—low-keyed but expensive style, and she always had to wear stockings and a bra!

Contextual boundaries help you to be more flexible and have more choices. If you are more congruent with your environment and show yourself in the most positive light, your resources will be more fully available to you.

> Once upon a time a Samurai goes to a Monk and says, "Monk, teach me about heaven and hell." The monk looks up at this huge Samurai and he says, "Teach *you* all about heaven and hell? I suppose you think you're special? You're dirty, you smell, your blade is rusty. Who would hire a Samurai like you? You're ugly. You're terrible. You're stupid. I couldn't teach you anything. Get away from me."
>
> The Samurai, with his neck muscles bulging, his blood vessels almost bursting in fury and rage, whips out his sword to kill the monk. Just as he is about to cut off the monk's head with his sword, the monk looks up at him and says, "That's hell."
>
> And the Samurai realizes that the monk has almost sacrificed his life to give him that teaching. He is so overwhelmed by the courage and compassion of the monk in doing what he had just done that he puts his sword back in its scabbard and bows in incredible appreciation of the beauty of that courage and compassion. He says to the monk, "I can't believe you just did that, risked your life to teach me."
>
> The monk replies, "And that's heaven."

Chapter V

Patterns Necessary to Support Boundaries

This chapter analyzes the five psychological developmental patterns that support the creation and maintenance of human boundaries: 1. Ego Strength, 2. Self as a Process, 3. Ability to Empathize, 4. Noticing Difference, 5. Observer Self. Only as we mature into adulthood do these patterns become stable and consistent—resulting in our ability to "do" boundaries choicefully and dependably.

Although Internal/External Boundaries begin to form soon after birth, Self/Other Boundaries around 4 to 6 months, and Contextual Boundaries around 4 years of age, initially these boundaries are quite primitive. It is not until you have developed certain cognitive and perceptual patterns that your boundaries become stable, flexible, consistent, and dependable. As you will see, these patterns develop over time, taking until your twenties and sometimes thirties to fully mature. This is why children cannot and do not maintain consistent boundaries. Unfamiliar, emotional, difficult, and traumatic events in the external environment overwhelm children, and their emotional and perceptual boundaries collapse. If the external circumstances are particularly painful, they will retreat behind a wall.

The five patterns necessary to maintain stable boundaries are *Ego Strength, Self as a Process, Ability to Empathize, Noticing Difference,* and *Observer Self.*

1. Ego Strength

The first pattern, Ego Strength, is a sense of self as a separate, unique individual. By the time you reach your twenties, you have a strong sense of what music you like, what kind of clothes you want to wear, and what you would describe as a "good time." How do you know these things? Over the years, you have had experiences that accumulate to form various values. Every value has two sides: one that you move toward and one that you move away from. Examples include strength/weakness and honesty/lying. These values become the standard against which you evaluate your present experience to determine whether something is good/bad or desirable/not desirable. This process begins at birth or before as the most fundamental value of pleasure/pain. You move toward pleasure and away from pain. This value is quickly joined by safety/danger. These two basic values are established through your experiences. Being held, touched, and fed is comforting; being rocked is pleasing; and being wet, cold, or hungry is unpleasant, even painful. Through these experiences, you begin to create emotional, perceptual, and physical definitions of pleasure and pain, safety and danger. These become the standards against which you evaluate new experiences. As you grow, these values become more and more refined and sophisticated, developing into other values: fun/boring, pretty/ugly, smart/stupid, successful/failure, and many others that are idiosyncratic to the individual.

What kinds of experience determine the formation of your values? There is always some external event, but is your value dependent upon the external circumstances *or* your internal experience in response to the external event, or a mix of both? For example, as you have developed your values about music, have they been formed as a result of what your peers like, what is "cool" at the moment, or what you feel about certain music, your internal response to it? This internal/external location is the frame of reference for your values. When you're very young, your values are mostly external. Therefore, you have primarily an external frame of reference. Pleasure comes from someone else touching you, holding you, singing to you, feeding you, playing with you. As you grow, other people's applause and approval make you feel good, and when Mom is angry at you, you feel that the world is coming to an end. For the first six years of life, most of your values come from your parents; you are dependent on them for your sense of well-being. As you move out into the world, you begin to assign importance to others such as teachers and friends. By the time you're a teenager, your peers, your particular heroes and heroines—those that your circle of friends have anointed as "cool" and worthy of adulation—have become the vessels of your values.

I remember when my youngest son was 13 and we went clothes shopping. He happened to look good in most clothes, but the ones he picked were not the ones that looked best on him or, God forbid, were the most comfortable. Oh, no! The clothes he had to have were the labels that his friends were wearing. And sneakers! What determined which sneakers he bought was not looks, comfort, or price; it was the brand that his "gang" was wearing. No wonder marketers aim so much of their advertising efforts at adolescents and teenagers. Their values no longer come from their parents but they are still external: what the other kids and their heroes are doing, listening to, and wearing. The external bombardment of advertising has that much more impact when the target's frame of reference is also external.

As you mature, your external values and standards get tempered by your inner responses to experiences. They become modified by your feelings and your sense of what's important, separate from what your friends or parents think is important. Gradually, you form your own unique emotional definition of values that become the standard against which you evaluate yourself, others, and the world. It's not that you abandon any and all external standards, as some are useful and beneficial in certain circumstances. When you're in a learning situation, it's more beneficial to use your teacher as your external standard. Choose a teacher with your own inner values, then use him or her as the way to evaluate your progress. Continue this until you're ready to move from the learning phase to the doing phase, when you begin to use your own developing inner values. Taking feedback is another example of the benefit of some external frame of reference. You can choose to modify your behavior because of someone else's sensitivity, even though you know—based upon your inner values—that your behavior is not wrong or bad.

At some point, you begin to choose music not just because that's what everyone in your social circle is listening to but because it's what you like. You discover that you like to listen to Bach as well as Madonna or Dave Matthews. The same is true for clothes; you wear what you think looks good on you and is comfortable, not

51

just what's in style that season. When you're able to decide to stay home on a Saturday night with a good book, knowing it's not because you don't have a date but because you want to, even though many of your friends are going to another new club, you're developing a strong internal frame of reference and a set of inner values. This creates a cradle for your sense of self, a connection to your inner essence that is unique and separate from the rest of the world yet capable of connecting deeply to others and the world. Only when you have a strong sense of self, a strong ego, can you choose to put it aside and enter an "egoless" state, which is both appropriate and effective in contexts such as teaching, counseling, mediating, coaching, and supervising.

2. Self as a Process

The second pattern is Self as a Process. Have you ever noticed that when you get stuck in a self-blaming loop, when you make a mistake and you can't stop beating yourself up, time seems to stand still. There's no real sense of the future, not in the true meaning of the concept. The future by definition is different from the present and the past: of course, there are similarities between the past, present, and future, but there has to be that gut realization that the future is going to be different; otherwise it doesn't qualify as the "future." When you're stuck in the beating-up-self loop, it feels as though it's always going to be this way, that you'll always mess up like this. Have you ever noticed that when you're depressed, the future looks black or exactly the same as right now—which is awful? This experience is a phenomenon of your relationship with Time with a capital T. When you experience yourself and Time as static, not moving, not changing, totally in the moment, you are "In Time." Sometimes this state is great: when you're making love, watching a sunset, at a concert, or teaching. There are many occasions when you want to be In Time because it deepens and accentuates the sensory and emotional experience, but there are just as many times when you want to be "Through Time." This is when you experience yourself as continually changing, as infinitely capable of evolving. Time is constantly moving and changing, and everything in the time–space continuum is affected by this. Even the ancient redwoods change over time. It is your relationship with Time that enables you to perceive and experience yourself as a dynamic, ever-moving, ever-changing process.

When you know yourself in this way, you can readily identify the future as different from the present and the past, because you are changing even as you move into the future. The one certainty we know is that tomorrow you will be different, the world will be different, and therefore anything is possible. Sometimes that's scary, especially when you're happy. When you have something you want, such as a relationship, approval, or success, you want your world to stay that way forever. The idea of change itself can be disquieting because it's unfamiliar and unpredictable, but trying to escape the inevitability of change is like trying to stop the movement of the stars and the planets.

Now consider that you are a verb! Even though grammatically "you" is a noun, defined as an object, a thing (a chair, a telephone), or a finished event (a wedding), are you a finished event? An object? I don't think so! A verb is a description of a process that is moving and changing. Are you a dynamic, moving, changing phenomenon? Are you a process? You certainly are! So *you are a verb!* You are a process! This is the second pattern necessary in order to maintain boundaries. You have the choice to experience yourself in relation to Time as an ever-moving, ever-changing process for whom anything is possible. No matter what happens to you, because there is always a future that is different from now (and then), you *can* learn, evolve, and grow and do it differently next time. A student of mine once told me, "There's no such thing as failure, only not enough time."

Think of how In Time children are. Have you ever taken a long car trip (or even a one-hour trip) with a 4 year old? "Are we there yet, Mommy?" "No, we have another hour to go." Five minutes later, you hear, "Mommy, are we there yet?" "No, another 55 minutes." And so it goes for the entire trip! Or have you ever been frustrated when trying to motivate your teenage son to start working on his term paper two weeks before it's due? "I've got plenty of time, Dad," he says, right up to a day before the deadline.

Children, adolescents, and teenagers have difficulty delaying gratification. There's a party tonight, and all your daughter Carol's friends are going. It doesn't matter that she has an important test the next day. She wants what she wants when she wants it—now! Instant gratification! Being In Time promotes instant gratification. Time stands still; only now exists, no past, no future. As with Ego Strength, you develop the capability to be Though Time as you mature. In Time can either blur distinctions within a static, unchanging time frame or wall off a period of time from the rest of experience. Through Time facilitates the permeability of boundaries, which supports the experience of self as a process. It allows connection with separation between the three different time frames: past, present, and future.

3. Ability to Empathize

The third pattern needed in maintaining boundaries is the ability to change your point of view, to "step into someone else's shoes" and experience the world through that person's eyes and ears, allowing you to identify with her, with her feelings. This is called empathy. To empathize with someone is not to merge with that person, lose your boundaries and your sense of self, but to shift your perspective to that of the other and imagine how she or he is feeling. This is very different from becoming the other. You maintain your own identity, but you shift your consciousness and your attention out of your model of the world and look at and listen to the world from another's point of view. It means giving up, at least for a moment, your place at the center of your world and figuratively stepping into someone else's.

I worked with a woman named Alicia who had very difficult interactions with her mother. She wanted to change this pattern, but she was very angry with her mother because she felt that her mother was always trying to tell her what to do and was very critical of what she did. I asked her to put herself in her mother's place and imagine a typical scene between the two of them. She began to realize that her mother was sad because she now felt so much on the periphery of her daughter's life. In contrast, when Alicia was a child, her mother was central to her life. Alicia began to understand that her mother was anxious to be included in her life, and these feelings drove her mother's bossy and critical behavior. This understanding helped Alicia to be kinder to her mother and sometimes ask for her opinion or advice. This soothed her mother and allowed her to relax, and Alicia allowed herself to benefit from her mother's wisdom. Their interactions were much more comfortable after that, and their relationship became more loving. Alicia learned to empathize with her mother rather than fight her.

When you read a story of a man whose house has burned to the ground, you can empathize or identify with his feelings. The loss of a home, familiar objects and beloved keepsakes, photographs, books, and old letters, is devastating. Even if the exact same thing has never happened to you, you can imagine what it would be like, and how you would feel. You therefore understand better how this man must feel. Changing your point of view to that of another increases your understanding of the other and allows you to empathize. For instance, imagine how helpful it would be to step into the shoes of a member of your family who is converting to a very different religion and to be able to see his decision from his point of view. This does not mean that you're going to agree with him or even like what he's doing, but you'll understand him better. He'll get the message that you at least respect that he's entitled to his beliefs. If you had a colleague at work who disagreed with how you were handling a particular problem, you would appreciate it if he showed his willingness to see your point of view even though he continued to disagree with you. You would feel acknowledged because he bothered to take the time to consider your viewpoint and develop empathy.

This pattern is about relinquishing the idea that you are the center of the universe. It is the realization that the world does not revolve around you. Other people have thoughts and feelings that are not the same as yours, do not depend on yours, and are not subordinate to yours. Children are rightfully the center of their universe, but as they mature, we hope that they will gradually give up this notion as they accept that other people's needs and wants are sometimes as important or more important than theirs. The ability to imagine yourself looking through another's eyes, hearing through another's ears, standing in another's body, and imagining how that person must feel and experience the world is necessary for a civilized society to exist. Mutual respect, appreciation, and compassion depend upon empathy. What prevents you from killing a stranger who offends you? Some might answer conscience, the rule of law, religious beliefs, but under all these is a human being's ability to identify with another's emotion. When civilization breaks down and people treat each other with unbelievable cruelty, I believe they have retreated behind walls where there is no connection, no more desire or ability to step into the other's shoes. Their capacity for empathy has been lost. When you shift your perspective to that of another person, you begin to realize how you are similar even when there are many differences. It is these real or imagined similarities that build mutual understanding. In the face of different cultures, religious beliefs, and values, you can empathize with a parent's grief over the death of a child.

I believe that this ability is fostered and nurtured by the early bonding that develops when an infant is held close to its mother's and father's body. Children who are not held as infants often grow up without the ability to empathize, to identify with others. Babies born to crack-addicted mothers are often also addicted; in some hospitals there are volunteers whose only job is to hold these infants—just to hold them!

The ability to identify with another human being's emotions is fundamental to your humanity. Empathy creates porousness in your ability to separate, and that in turn allows experience, emotions, and information to flow toward the other and from the other, sending energy out and receiving it back. You are connecting!

4. Noticing Difference

Donald W. Winnicott, noted British pediatrician, child psychoanalyst, teacher, and theorist, (1896–1971) said, "It is by difference that we grow" (from *Boundaries and Space. An Introduction to the Work of D. W. Winnicott,* by M. Davis & D. Wallbridge, 1991). What does that mean? What is *difference*? It is the ability to make distinctions between people, situations, or information, to notice when and how something is unlike something else. This depends on your ability to make comparisons and to generalize from them. When you compare two or more objects, people, situations, or information, you are looking for how they are similar and different.

The fourth pattern necessary to create and maintain boundaries is the ability to notice difference. In order to do this, you must be comparing, even on an unconscious level. You see how an apple and an orange are different, how your two neighbors are different, how a cocktail party is different from a class in graduate school. In noticing these differences, you make distinctions. You separate one thing from another, one person from another, or one situation from another. It is only by noticing differences that things, people, and situations become distinguishable from the general mush of experience. Only when they are separate and emerge from the background can you learn about them.

Your values and beliefs are refined and become your own only when put through the filter of difference. Say that your father believed that people must be responsible for their own life. At first you rebelled against his credo of responsibility, but as you matured you started to realize that he had a point. While accepting the validity of his premise, you began to test it in the crucible of your own personal experience. You noticed how his notion of responsibility was different from yours, how your feelings of responsibility were different from his. As you grew up, you accepted your similarities and molded your own beliefs about responsibility through difference.

It is only by making distinctions that you are able to label things and information. When everything is the same, it becomes like mush; all uniqueness, distinction, and meaning are lost. You end up with nothing. You may end up "overlabeling," becoming obsessed with the label itself and forgetting the experience that you are labeling. Labels are like handles: when something has a handle, you can more easily pick it up or pick it out of a mass of similar objects. Have you ever tried cooking with a pot that has no handles?

Think of your personal resources. You might count among them strength, fairness, honesty, beauty, and compassion. Consider that it is only when you can label and can make distinctions among your talents, abilities, attitudes that you can finally appreciate them and use them. When they stay hidden in a generalized mush, you can't get a hold of them when you need them.

Being able to compare and notice the difference between your creativity and your spontaneity makes each more real.

> A student of mine, Bernard, claimed that he had no resources. In spite of my clever questioning and metaphors, he remained steadfast in his claim. Finally at my wit's end, I asked him to tell me about something he did that he considered easy. He described how he told his children bedtime stories. He not only told the story but, with stuffed animals, pillows, blankets, and furniture, would create the actual environment of the story. Thus he would bring to life the jungle, the farm, the train station, the castle, wherever the story took place. The entire class and I were very impressed and thought that he was very creative in doing this. We loudly voiced our admiration, and Bernard finally began to accept his ability to be creative as he separated it from just doing his job as a parent. He started to see that what he did when telling his children their bedtime story was different from how most of us do it, and because it was different he had to examine it and label it. Once this resource had a handle, he could pick it up and put other experiences into this pot called creativity. By the end of the training, he realized that he had quite a few personal resources!

When you notice difference, you increase your awareness, expand your knowledge of the world, broaden your horizons, and develop your possibilities. This pattern enables you to see and hear and feel where you end and the external world begins. It helps you to learn how you are different from others and how others are different from you and each other. As with most interesting phenomena in life, there is a paradox here. In order to notice difference, you must be aware of sameness. At the same time, it is essential that you can be comfortable with difference, even embrace difference rather than try to always make things the same. When you attempt to fit everything together, accepting only the familiar, you'll miss the opportunities and expansion that difference brings. You'll shrink instead of grow.

5. Observer Self

The fifth pattern needed for building boundaries is the ability to develop an Observer Self: a self that can step back, watch, listen, and have feelings *about* yourself. This self can separate from sensory immediacy (sight, sound, smell, taste, and sensation) that engulfs you in emotions and observe without participating. It is as though you become a fly on the wall, observing yourself looking through the lens of a camera, watching and listening to yourself interacting with others and being in the world.

With this ability, you become more aware of yourself in relation to others and begin to see the big picture of which you are a part. This pattern certainly demonstrates that you are not the center of the universe but only a player. "All the world's a stage and all the men and women merely players." (*As You Like It*, William Shakespeare)

> Imagine that you are caught up in the emotion of a fight with your lover. You are devastated by his cruelty. Instead of sympathizing with your plight of the moment: the apparent betrayal of your dearest friend who would rather visit her new friends than come to see you this weekend. You are hurt and afraid that your friend doesn't care for you as much as you'd thought. And when you tell your lover about your misery, what does he do? He points out that you're being petty and self-centered, that your friend has a right to make new friends and expand her social circle. You can't believe that he would take her side and deliberately say such nasty things!
>
> Now imagine that you take a deep breath, a figurative step back from yourself, and become your Observer Self. You watch and listen to yourself and your lover. You notice that you look and sound very angry, even at the beginning of the discussion! Your voice is very loud, your tone is harsh, and you're speaking so fast and continuously that your lover has no time or space to say a word. Then you yell at him for not saying anything comforting! Your face looks like you were sucking on a lemon: mouth puckered, brows drawn together, and eyes squinty. You also observe that—at least from this observer's point of view—your lover at first looked concerned and tried to say something to comfort you. He was looking at you and nodding his head. When he spoke, his voice was quiet, and he used words like, "I'm sorry you're so upset and . . ." You kept interrupting him and spoke louder and louder and began to blame him for not caring about how you were feeling.

It's not that you don't have a right to be disappointed by your friend not coming to visit you or to want some sympathy from your lover, but *how* you told him about the situation had a lot to do with how he responded to you. If you had lowered your volume and had given him some room to say something, you might have gotten the comfort you wanted.

By stepping into the Observer Self, you got another perspective on the situation and your behavior. You were able, for a moment, to move out of the whirlwind of your emotions and learn something about yourself. You could see the big picture of the entire interaction, not just your emotional side of it. Getting more information you became aware of other choices. It is important to recover your boundaries with your friend. She is a separate individual, and she has the right to a life separate from yours. You assumed that she doesn't care about you because she's visiting other friends (loss of boundaries at the Internal/External Boundary level in the category of Causality—"friend visiting others" means "betrayal"). Additionally, you mixed your lover and your friend together. When he didn't immediately respond exactly the way you wanted him to, you lost the distinction between him and your feelings about your friend (Self/Other Boundaries). You were mind-reading, assuming that if he didn't respond in a certain way, it meant that he didn't care about you. By stepping into the Observer Self position, you saw and heard information that reminded you that you and your lover are separate individuals—and that you don't always precisely know what he's thinking and feeling.

You don't want to remain in Observer Self all the time. The position is one of observing, rather than fully participating. It is helpful in getting more information about yourself and yourself in relation to the entire situation. It puts you above the wave of emotion of an experience so that you can learn something, but most of the time you want to participate in your life, not live it as an observer. This is a choice—an important one, but still a choice—depending on circumstances.

As these patterns form, they create the foundation for reliable and flexible boundaries. These cognitive and perceptual patterns develop over time as a result of your experience and your maturation.

Although children have a simple and basic sense of boundaries, without the development of these patterns, their boundaries easily collapse in the face of unfamiliar or painful external events. Boundaries can be considered the ultimate resource, because if you had had stable boundaries as a child, you would have made fewer negative decisions about who you are, what you're capable of, and what the world is.

Once upon a time, there was an anthropologist who discovered a lost tribe living far from civilization. The people of this tribe were friendly and kind and seemed very wise. In spite of the fact that the man's inner confusion and unhappiness was disturbing to their harmony, they accepted and made him feel welcome.

He befriended one of the inhabitants of a small village. One day this friend took him to the top of a high cliff overlooking a fast-moving and tumultuous river with a small island in the middle of it. There was a calm, mysterious beauty about the island, but it seemed impossible to reach. Dangerous currents and whirlpools swirled around the island, and there was no bridge from either shore. The water looked too dangerous even for boats. The man gazed for a long time at this island and was curiously moved; he felt that it was his destiny to visit this island.

After a time, another man climbed down the cliff over a barely visible path and stood quietly on the edge of the shore. Eventually a rainbow appeared and seemed to make a beautiful bridge from the shore to the island. The anthropologist was amazed when the man on the shore put his foot on the rainbow and crossed over to the island!

"How did he do that?" he asked his friend. "It is very simple. You just need to know your color. Put your feet exactly on that color, and you will be able to cross over." The anthropologist was very excited because he thought he had found the answer to fulfilling his destiny and visiting the island. He said to his friend, "You are a very wise man and surely you can tell me: what is *my* color?" His friend said that that was not possible. "The color is inside you, and only you can discover it. However, I can help you to find the way."

The anthropologist was impatient and kept asking "How? What must I do?" His friend explained that he must study, read, and meditate and that he would bring him to other wise people who could guide him, but he said, "Only *you* can find your color."

And so the anthropologist worked with the wise people of the village, studied and meditated, and after many, many months, he felt he was ready to try to reach the island. With his friend, he climbed down the cliff path to the edge of the shore, looked across to that special, magical island, and waited patiently. Soon a rainbow appeared and made a bridge to the island. He put his foot on the color that he recognized as his and, yes, he crossed the river on that rainbow to the island of his destiny. He spent many days exploring the island, finding it full of marvelous colors, the colors of all the wise people who had visited before him. He finally understood that he had to leave his color here on the island, that very special and personal color it took him so long to find. But when he left, he knew that he would take away with him a little bit of the color of each wise person who had come before him.

Now he is truly finding harmony for himself and learning what wisdom is.

Adapted from a story by Patrick Condamin

Chapter VI

Doing Boundaries

This chapter provides a detailed description of the three ways we create and maintain boundaries: simultaneous thinking, connecting to our body, and peripheral seeing and hearing. The lack of or distortion of these learned skills can cause serious problems with our self-esteem, and in our relationships. Included in this chapter are simple exercises to strengthen these skills.

Now that you have an idea of what boundaries are, the different levels of boundaries, and the developmental patterns necessary to support boundaries, you're probably asking yourself, "What can I do with this information? How can it make a difference in my life?" This chapter will answer that question.

You're already doing boundaries, but you're not aware of what you're doing or how you're doing it. Since you're not aware, you have few choices about creating and maintaining boundaries: when, where, with whom.

When I first started showing my Irish Wolfhounds in the breed ring, they sometimes looked great and sometimes they didn't. After taking some handling classes, I became aware that the size of the steps I was taking when I moved the dogs around the ring made a difference in how they reached out with their front feet and drove with their rear feet. I also learned where to put their feet when they were standing to make them look their best for the judge. Now I have more choice because I'm aware of *how* to show an Irish Wolfhound rather than accidentally getting it right sometimes and at other times making a mess, and not knowing what made the difference, only the results.

Boundaries are not something you have, like dark hair or a car. They are the result of the type of filters you use to organize your experience. You have three primary types of filters: cognitive (simultaneous thinking), physiological (connecting to your body), and perceptual (your peripheral vision and hearing). The ways you use these filters become the skills of "doing" boundaries. They are the "how-tos" of boundaries. Filters are like strainers. For example, you're at the beach, and you want to collect small, round pebbles, medium-sized square pebbles, and orange pebbles. You have a strainer that has small, round holes, medium-sized square holes, and holes that let only orange pebbles through. Now there are millions of differently shaped and colored pebbles in the sand that you are sifting, but because of this special strainer, as you sift you will only collect the pebbles that are small and round, medium-sized and square, or orange.

Your conscious mind does this same sort of sifting. Because your conscious mind is very limited, it must select for particular kinds of information. It can only pay attention to between five and nine pieces of information at any moment. This means that you could not walk across a room if you had to do everything consciously: if you had to consciously monitor every shift in weight, contraction and expansion of muscles, lifting, flexing, and movement, there would not be enough conscious attention available to accomplish the simple task of walking. Your unconscious mind compares incoming information with the information and experiences you already have stored. It creates categories, generalizations, and sequences, and it stores these for future use. How does your limited conscious mind deal with the bombardment of thousands or millions of data in any experience? Like the strainer selecting for pebbles of a certain size, shape, and color, the mind also has filters. It selects for certain types of information and thus creates an attitude, mood, receptivity, or resistance. Think of bamboo blinds or thin, cotton, gauzy curtains and how they filter the light coming through a window. Imagine a room with no blinds, how the sun streams in creating brightness, warmth, and clarity. When you put bamboo blinds on the windows, what happens to the mood of that room? The light is darker, cooler, and more diffused. The blinds or the curtains do not block out the light entirely but filter it in ways that change the ambiance of the environment. Light coming through a blue or green or red curtain, or through a light or dark bamboo blind, creates very different effects. The same effect happens when different-colored filters are put on the lights of a movie set or theater stage; they set the mood for the scene unfolding before the audience.

> Consider a day when you wake up in a good mood. You're think-ing about the attractive girl you're having dinner with later and the papers you finished marking last night that you'll return to your students today. It's raining outside, and it reminds you of the foggy, misty, romantic atmosphere of London. When you pick up your morning coffee and paper at the local café, the guy behind the counter is very busy so you tip him extra and get a big smile from him. "What a great day to be alive! Everything's coming up roses!" On another morning, you wake up and the first thought you have is the fight you had the day before with your best friend. On top of that, you're overdrawn at the bank, your car insurance is due, and you're feeling like warm beer and burnt toast. It's raining—again! The world is gray and gloomy and depressing. That guy behind the counter keeps you waiting forever for your coffee, and when you ask him to hurry it up, he gives you attitude! So this is how the day's going to be: lousy!

The only difference between these two scenarios is your mindset. Your mental frame filters either for the positive or the negative and, once you start noticing what's wrong or what's right with the day, you become more and more aware of one to the exclusion of the other; this creates your mood. A mood is like being on a slide running downhill; you keep gathering momentum and it's difficult to change direction once you're on board.

1. Simultaneous Thinking

The cognitive filter of simultaneous thinking refers to the ability to notice sameness and difference equally rather than emphasizing one over the other. One is not better than the other, and neither is inherently positive or negative. They're just different ways of organizing information.

Have you ever noticed that some people constantly say things such as, "That's the same as ..." or "She's like ..." or "This is similar to ..." These people primarily pay attention to how something or someone is the same as something else they've experienced. They experience the world in terms of similarities and sameness. Others experience the world through differences; they look, listen, and feel for what doesn't fit or is missing. They tend to use phrases such as, "Yes, but" or "Except for" or "Not quite" and "Not completely." They pay attention mostly to how things are different from each other. When you're learning something new, do you think about how the material is similar to other models you've learned or how it's different? With memories, do you notice the same aspects of a memory each time you think of it, or do you become aware of different details? One of the most basic and essential functions of your mind is the ability to compare, to notice sameness and difference. On a deep unconscious level, you compare the situation, the information, and the people with what you've already experienced. When you compare two chairs, you might notice how they're similar in size and type: both have flower-pattern upholstery, wooden legs, and are comfortable. Or you might notice how they're different: the texture of one is silky smooth and the other is rough with a deep pile, the back of one is higher than that of the other, one is more predominantly red while the other has more greens and blues, and the red one has a straighter back, which makes it more comfortable for a longer period of time, and so on.

What happens when you concentrate on one to the exclusion of the other? Let's suppose that you are meeting someone for the first time, and you are interested in getting to know this person better.

> Imagine a scenario in which you are primarily noticing sameness. You're aware that you're both women, you are both thin, and you both wear glasses. You have the same family background: middle class, white, suburban, and married with two children. You both can get depressed easily and have trouble asserting yourself. You're both worried about future security and are frightened about the conflicts that are happening in the world. At first you are very comfortable with this new friend; it seems you have similar thoughts and very similar feelings and beliefs. It's as though you've met yourself. You begin to see each other often. The problem is that when she's depressed, you get depressed, and when you're worried, she gets worried. You seem to strengthen each other's moods and outlook on life, including the negative, which can get both depressing and boring. What if your similarity was that you were both happy-go-lucky and always looked on the bright side? Even

then, if you were mostly paying attention to how you were the same, there would be no room for you to feel another emotion like sadness or fear, and that could get frustrating. In both cases, you're losing boundaries.

When a person's entire mental frame is sameness, she can be threatened by difference. She may think, "What do you mean you're changing and evolving? I want you to stay the same as when I met you, the same as when I fell in love with you." Or, "We've always been happy together. What do you mean you're worried or angry?" Excessive sameness encourages merging and losing individual boundaries.

> Let's reconsider the scenario of meeting a new friend, this time with the emphasis on difference. You notice that you're younger and taller than she is and that she wears her hair in an old-fashioned bun, whereas you style yours in the latest spiky fashion. She wears a slip under her skirt and stockings; you don't wear slips and never put on stockings unless it's below freezing. Her parents are still together, and yours have both remarried several times. You have a graduate degree, and she just finished high school. Her kids never sleep over at friends or have a regular bedtime hour, while yours are very social and go to bed at a specific time. You're determined to be successful and secure a future for yourself and your family; you want to help change the world, to make a difference in some way; she concentrates on creating a safe world for her family. Her approach to a frightening world is to give in to her fears while you get angry. She lets everyone know about her depression while you never publicly admit to getting depressed.

Are these two women going to develop a close relationship? When you mostly notice difference, you're creating walls through which you're not going to be able to connect, because to connect you need some commonality. When your mental frame is only difference, you can give the impression of being argumentative and disagreeable even though that's not your intention—it's just how you think. Excessive difference builds walls and prevents connection.

You have a choice: to notice sameness *or* difference, or sameness *and* difference. This skill applies also to your internal experience. If you primarily concentrate on the same thoughts and feelings, it's great when you're happy and doing well, but disastrous when you've had a serious failure or disappointment. You'll think, "It's always going to be like this, tomorrow, next week, next month." "My life will be the same forever as it is today." (This pattern also applies to your memories.)

> I worked with a woman, Helen, on her issues with holidays, especially Christmas. She dreaded this holiday, but she couldn't just ignore it because it was an important day for her husband. He had grown up in a family that made it very special and happy, and he wanted to continue that tradition with their children. Because Helen hated Christmas so much, she never had a good time and always seemed to provoke a fight or something unpleasant. We explored her experiences of Christmas as a child, which she described as bleak, lonely, and unhappy. Her parents always seemed to get into a fight; her father drank too much, her mother spent too much money, and each constantly harped on the faults of the other.
>
> As Helen was an only child, she felt very alone with these two warring adults and had no one with whom to commiserate. As we explored these memories, they were always exactly the same: the images, the feelings, and the disapproving words and tone of her parents never changed. I asked her to pick one of these early memories of Christmas, go through it again, and notice anything different about the memory. Did she see, feel, or hear anything different? I kept emphasizing the possibility of seeing or hearing something different, something she hadn't remembered before. After a while, she reported hearing voices coming from the kitchen and realized that it was her aunt and uncle helping to prepare the Christmas meal. She had totally forgotten that they used to spend the holiday with her and her parents every year until she was about 9, when they moved to another state far away. She also remembered that those Christmases had had some happy moments. Her aunt and uncle were cheerful, warm, and affectionate people who loved her and demonstrated their love. Helen's impression of Christmas had been absolute and negative, and her mental frame was that of sameness. Whenever she thought of Christmas, it was through the same negative images, sounds, and feelings she'd always remembered. It was as though she'd rehearsed her memories of Christmas until every word, image, and feeling was set in stone. I asked her to notice anything that was different from what she'd always assumed

to be the "real" experience, and this changed her present attitude toward Christmas. Now everything about her childhood memories was not negative; there had been some positive moments. This step created some internal space to support the possibility of enjoying Christmas and creating a happy time for herself and her family.

What affect can an unconscious habit of primarily noticing differences have on memories? For instance, you have wonderful childhood memories of spending summers at the beach with your entire family. However, every time you think of these times and begin to feel those warm, happy, safe feelings, you think of how it all changed when you were a teenager. Your parents divorced, your older brother was away in the Army, and money was a constant worry. Now it's even worse: your father is dead, your brother moved to the other coast, your sister is married to an obnoxious slob, and your mother sold the house at the beach. Your entire family is scattered and hardly ever gets together anymore in one place at one time. In this case, your excessive attention to difference robs you of the pleasure of the earlier, happy memories by walling off those feelings. When you emphasize difference, you can't hold on to the positive aspects of yourself and your experience. It's as though you're compelled to think about what's not the same. This works well when you're unhappy or have had a failure, but it does not serve you in positive circumstances, nor does it help to build self-esteem or confidence. You want to notice both sameness *and* difference in a harmonious way.

Harmony between sameness *and* difference is not having balance between the two. Balance is a polarized and static state. Something is either in balance or out of balance, there's nothing in-between. Think of an old-fashioned type of scale, with two surfaces on top of a balancing arm. When you put exactly equal weights on each side, they maintain balance, but nothing can move. If it does, the balance is broken. Even a breeze can throw off the balance. Harmony describes movement from one place to the other—the flow of water moving from one space to another, the movement of sound from one pitch, volume, and tempo to another, the harmonious flow of energy from one person to another. Think of two people who have a harmonious relationship: they do not keep score, counting the times one or the other wins an argument, the times when one is needy and dependent and the other is strong.

The wins, losses, weaknesses, strengths, control, and power flow between them. They are not counted in numbers but experienced as a loving and respectful flow. You have probably had a friend of whom you were fond, but after a while, you got more and more upset with her because of her self-centeredness. Whenever you were together, all she seemed to talk about was herself, and this went on for years. Even when you were hurting or very happy and wanted to talk about it, she would always bring the conversation back around to her own life. Would it have resolved the problem satisfactorily if you got 60 minutes to talk about yourself and then she got 60 minutes to talk about herself? Or that one time you met, she was the center of attention, and the next time it was your turn? That would have been balanced, but would you have enjoyed it? Would you have felt good about the relationship? Probably not. Although balanced, the solution is static and artificial. In a relationship you want a flow, a back and forth, not based on quantity but on quality.

One of the how-tos of doing boundaries is noticing sameness and difference simultaneously, and this is the cognitive filter of simultaneous thinking. You can practice this consciously. Several times each day, ask yourself, "Am I noticing how this situation is the same as I expected it to be or how it is different?" "Am I aware of feeling the same about this person as I usually do, or am I feeling different?" "Am I thinking about this information the same way or differently than I usually do?" When you meet someone new, be aware of what you're noticing. Perhaps you pick up on how you're both in the same profession or how different your accents are.

You can practice this skill by working through the following tasks:

1. Pick a situation you know is coming up. Set the goal of noticing five things that are the same as they've always been and five things that are different from what you've noticed before or expected. Do this three times a week, and schedule it into your appointment book.

2. Keep a notebook of sameness AND difference. Write down some things you've noticed that are the same as always or are the same as what you expected, and a couple that are different

from what you've noticed before or are different from your expectations. Do this every day for a week. Read what you've written at the end of the week. Which way, sameness or difference, is easier and more familiar? The way that is more difficult is the one you want to work on!

3. A couple times a week, think about a particular memory, and determine each time whether you're noticing that things are the same or different. Are the images, words, and feelings the same as usual, or are you aware of differences in the memory—differences compared to another memory or differences compared to now? When this type of task becomes easier, pick a mildly unpleasant memory, and notice whether your mental frame is one of sameness OR difference. Then deliberately change your frame. If you've been noticing sameness, notice what's different, and if you've been noticing what's different, notice what's the same.

Practicing your awareness of these frames and developing flexibility in changing them will increase your choices and develop an essential boundary skill.

2. Connecting to Your Body

What do I mean by that? You might think that everybody is connected to their body. After all, I can look down and see my hands and legs, and I know they're my hands and legs. I know they're connected to my body and that they belong to me, not someone else. Of course, you know your arms are connected to your torso and your feet are connected to your legs. You know that your feet and the ground are different and that your arms and your shirt are different. Is that all you need to connect to your body, to know intellectually that this is your body? Connecting to your body means more than just knowing on a cognitive level. It means knowing in your gut, being tuned in to your body, being aware of small and large shifts in contractions, expansions, temperature, pressure, moisture, inner movements, and vibrations. It means a flow and a harmony between your thoughts and your physical sensations. This is your physiological filter.

Your entire body is a filter for your experience. When a person smiles, the physiological changes in the facial muscles, the shaping of the lips, and the movement of the skin results in the person feeling better! Even if you don't feel happy or pleased just before you smile, when you do smile, the physiological movements of a smile make you feel better. Try it out for yourself; when you're in a grumpy mood, allow yourself to smile at the slightest excuse. Even help your face along by deliberately smiling at someone who is just passing you by or at the spring flowers by the side of the road, or a floppy-eared puppy. Rather than waiting for the internal emotion of a smile to cause the external response of smiling, do the smile first. Does it make a difference?

It's not just smiles that make a difference. Try thinking of something positive: a memory, an idea, or a goal while you're slumped over with your chin in your chest, your head bent down, your shoulders hunched forward, and your midsection caved in. Can you do it? It's impossible! Have you ever seen a depressed person with his head up, ribcage lifted, and weight centered in the pelvis? "Keep your chin up" is a cliché you say to someone when you want to encourage him to be brave, to believe that things will work out. There's literally truth in that saying. Your posture creates a body attitude, a mood that affects your thinking and emotions. Not only does good posture make you look good to others, but it makes you look good to yourself. It makes you feel better and think better.

Being connected to your body is a skill that is essential to creating and maintaining boundaries. Connecting to your body means believing that you can think *and* feel, experiencing a connection, rather than putting a wall between your head and your body. When you vividly imagine yourself at the beach soaking up the hot sun, your body actually begins to feel warmer. When a person who is allergic to pollen starts to think about being in a pine forest in June, when the pollen is so heavy it coats everything with a thick yellow film, his nose and eyes can actually start to run—even though he's indoors and it's snowing outside.

Your thoughts affect your body, and your body affects your thoughts. They are separate but inseparable. Your physical sensations are an integral part of your thinking process. Thinking consists of images, sounds, words, and sensations. Connecting to your body demands being aware of your physical sensations—and honoring and valuing them. Some sensations are pretty obvious: moving your feet, clenching your hands, lifting your arms, jumping, stepping, feeling the texture of a piece of fleece or silk or rough wool. When you touch something smooth, you're aware of that sensation in your fingers, and it can give you pleasure.

What about the less-obvious feelings such as the body sensations that let you know you've had enough to eat or drink? Are you aware of the signals, and do you honor them? Do you pay attention to them and respond appropriately? Or are you oblivious, ignoring them and continuing to eat or drink until you're so full that you're actually in distress? Being full is a pleasurable feeling, but some people don't recognize their body's message of fullness until they're in pain. For them, full is the same as being bloated and physically uncomfortable or, worse, passing out. Why? They're not tuned in to their body, not connected enough to recognize and acknowledge the body's signals. What are the specific sensations of being pleasantly full? The next time you eat a good meal, stop before you have seconds or dessert, and ask yourself what you are feeling in your body. Is there a sensation of expansion and warmth in your belly, a stillness in your mid- and lower chest? What do you feel?

Your body talks to you, and the language it uses is sensation. It is important to take the time to learn this language and then listen and respond. Do you know when you're tired and need to sleep, or does it take a migraine to get you in bed? There's a difference between being tired and wanting to escape. Do you recognize the sensations in your body that tell you this? Understanding the language of your body empowers you to appreciate these kinds of distinctions. Your body is an equal partner with your mind and your soul in this journey of the self.

The examples I've so far given are about physical phenomena. What about emotions? An emotion is an idea or concept closely associated with a physical sensation. Some people think emotions are like aliens from outer space: they can land on you without any logic or any warning, for any reason. According to this theory, you are a victim of your emotions. They're not connected to you until they hit you, and then the primary connection is the impact they have on you! In other words, you have no choice about your emotions! Let's consider the definition of an emotion: an idea or concept connected to a physical sensation, which is then labeled as an emotion. The idea could be something external to you: seeing someone hit his dog or smile at you, hearing the sound of wind chimes, a siren, or a person shouting. It could be the smell of fresh bread baking that takes you back to your grandmother's kitchen, the first taste of a cold beer on a summer day at the ocean, or the texture of a baby's hand in yours. These external sensory experiences have an impact on you, and you experience some sort of physical sensation, which you label as *anger, pleasure,* or *love.* Perhaps, when you see someone hit his dog, you feel tightness in your stomach and heat in your head. You might label this as *anger*, and you respond accordingly. A siren could elicit a sinking sensation in your stomach or a contraction in your chest that makes you hold your breath; you might call that *fear*. The smell of bread baking brings a feeling of expansion through your torso and up into your head and could be called *pleasure*.

Your internal visual and auditory experiences affect your body as much as the external ones. You imagine your boss looking at you with approval or your mother-in-law scowling at you, or the words of your lover when he told you he was leaving you, or the song that you played on your car tape deck the summer you turned 18. The memories of your experiences present themselves as images, sounds, words, textures, smells, and tastes; they evoke a physical sensation that your unconscious labels with a descriptive word that describes an emotion and which you experience as an emotion. What you see, hear, touch, smell, or taste in the external world or your inner world combines with the physical sensation and results in what you call an emotion.

Consider how obvious this concept is with very intense emotions. For instance, *anxiety.* You have a vague thought of impending doom that starts with the words "what if?" and a fluttering movement and pressure in your chest. *Despair* can start with an image of blackness, the words "It's always going to be like this," and the sensation of everything contracting into an empty hole in the middle of your body. Extreme *pleasure* can begin with certain images and smells accompanied by a lifting, vibrating movement that starts in the pelvis and moves up through the chest and into the head, a vibration in the back of your throat. A certain touch or smell might elicit a downward movement throughout your entire body, from the chest and stomach to the pelvis and buttocks, thighs, legs and toes, with a warm flush over most of the skin that could be called *ecstasy*. *Panic* is another emotion with a strong physiological component: you see, hear, and smell something extremely terrifying, and you feel tremendous pressure in your chest, to the extent that you can't breathe, and you feel chills run up and down your spine. You are in the emotional state of panic.

We are all familiar with the physiological sensations connected to intensely strong emotions, but what about all the other emotions we experience: responsibility, calmness, worry, satisfaction, contentment, irritation, concern, impatience, regret, envy, fairness, independence, and so on? What distinction does your body make between *concern* and *worry*? Do you recognize the sensation peculiar to each? Every emotion you experience has a sensation associated with it, and the more you expand your body's vocabulary, the clearer the flow of communication will be between your mind and body. You will develop great skill at "doing" boundaries.

The language of your body consists of a variety of physical sensations (vocabulary) that are shaped and made specific by the dynamics (grammar) of the body:

Vocabulary	Grammar
Pressure	Location
Release	Size
Movement	Direction
Vibration	Duration (continuity)
Expansion	Tempo (even/uneven)
Contraction	Intensity (strength)
Temperature (warm/cool)	Frequency
Moisture (wet/dry)	Consistency
Weight (heavy/light)	Difference

Use the grammar to make the vocabulary more specific. For example, where (location) is the sensation of expansion or contraction? In the stomach? Upper or lower chest? Head? Ears? Throat? Arms? Legs? Pelvis? Buttocks? Does the sensation begin small (size) and radiate (movement) outward, getting bigger (size), or begin

75

large and get smaller? Is the pressure heavy or light (weight)? Where (location) is it? Is it the same intensity over the entire area of pressure, or are the edges of it weaker than the center (consistency)? Does the movement flutter, flow, or beat? Where does it start and end (direction)?

To expand and deepen your connection to your body, practice the following:

1. Become more aware of your body. Direct your attention to the sensations of your body rather than your emotions. Your physical sensations are an important aspect of your thoughts. Recognize that you're not a "talking head" or a sensitive sponge. Your head and body are not severed at the neck; each serves a purpose in the harmony of thinking. Take the time to label different sensations as you become aware of them.

2. Sit quietly and remember something calming and pleasant; notice what is happening in your body and where it is happening. Use the above vocabulary and grammar to sharpen your awareness of and make each sensation more specific. Although there are some universal physiological responses to certain emotions like grief, with pressure and pain in the chest, or a slowing of movement and expansion in contentment, you are a unique individual with your own special response to specific circumstances. The point here is to get to know your body's language.

3. Take the time to sit with yourself and notice the changing sensations as you change your thoughts. Remember a mildly disturbing conversation you had with an employee, an amusing interaction with your grandchild, an unpleasant interaction with a salesperson, or the fireflies in the darkness of an early summer evening. The sensations are there—you just have to direct your attention to your body and ask yourself, "What body sensation am I feeling? What is happening inside me?" Remember to be patient with yourself. Do not try to force awareness; allow the sensations to make themselves known to you. They will do so when you give them the opportunity.

4. The next time you eat a good meal, before you take seconds or before your plate is completely clean, wait ten minutes, and notice the sensations in your body. Ask yourself questions and label these sensations. Compare them with the sensations you felt before you began to eat and when you stopped eating before waiting ten minutes.

5. Stand up and lift your rib cage, keeping your shoulders relaxed. Center your weight in your belly button, and take a deep, long breath. Hold that breath for ten seconds, and then exhale. Notice what happens in your body. Notice your physical sensations. Perhaps you've experienced some emotion that you want to let go of but you think you don't know how. Your body knows how; when you exhale you're letting go of your breath, and you do this thousands of times each day. The next time you begin to experience the emotion that you want to let go of, take a deep breath, hold it for six seconds, and then exhale, saying to yourself, "I'm letting go of ..." Repeat this several times.

6. Sit in a chair with both feet on the ground. Visualize your back. Notice how your back touches the back of the chair, and register the difference between your back and the chair. This "difference" determines where you begin and the chair ends. Put your hands on the chair arms, and feel the texture of the chair arm with your fingers. Say to yourself, "These are my hands and my arms on that chair, and they are connected to MY body." Feel your feet on the floor, feel your weight on your feet as you lean forward, feel the shift of weight as you lean back, lift your feet alternately up and down, stamp your foot a little bit as you put it down. Say to yourself, "This is my body, this is me sitting here in this chair."

7. Finally, notice whether you get nervous or scared when you connect more to your body. If you do, it means that a part of your unconscious has some objection to you doing this. This is not a bad sign; it is simply information that you need to successfully develop and maintain boundaries. That part of you that objects, that gets scared or angry, is trying to protect you in some way. (We will go into greater detail about this in Chapter 8.) For now, it is enough to realize you may have an

objection to fully connecting to your body. Acknowledge the objection, and to the best of your ability, appreciate that a part of you is trying to take care of you, even if you don't like how that part is doing it.

Remember to take your physical sensations into consideration whenever you're making a decision, learning, motivating yourself, being creative, or thinking. Ask yourself, "What am I sensing in my body?" Remember, too the famous saying of the French philosopher René Descartes (1596–1660), "I think, therefore I am." To many people, this means only intellectual, cognitive processing, and they forget or discount physical sensations.

Your head is not a computer sitting on a table, having nothing to do with your physical being. Your physical sensations are an integral part of your thinking and your intelligence. Honor them as the important contributions to your thinking that they are.

3. Peripheral Vision and Hearing

The third skill necessary to create and maintain boundaries is using the perceptual filters of peripheral vision and hearing. Look up from this page you're reading and direct your eyes to a small spot in front of you. Focus on that spot and, without moving your eyes, notice what else you can see besides the spot. Staying focused on the spot, see the colors, shapes, light and shadow, and movements to the right and the left of you. Put your hands up to about ear height, two to three feet from your head, and wiggle your fingers. Keep looking at that spot in front of you. Can you see your fingers moving? If you can, move them back a few inches until they're just on the edge of your vision. If you can't see your fingers, move them forward until you can. This is your peripheral vision: everything you can see without looking directly at it. Foveal vision is seeing what is immediately in front of you, while peripheral vision is the panoramic arc of your seeing. Peripheral hearing is being aware of the sounds all around you as well as those directly in front of you, as in stereophonic sound, rather than concentrating only on the sounds emanating from one source, as in monophonic sound. Two people who are intimately involved with each other can be in a noisy restaurant and be aware of nothing except the eyes, mouth, voice, words, and expressions of the other. If you asked them about the high decibel level around them, they would probably look at you blankly and say, "What noise?" They've happily lost their boundaries and their peripheral hearing. My research and experience indicate that peripheral vision is often easier and more effective for most people than peripheral hearing. You will find a certain emphasis in this book on peripheral vision, but this is not intended to discount those of you for whom peripheral hearing has more impact.

Long ago, our ancestors spent a great deal of time walking on trails through jungles, forests, and deserts. There were no street lamps or headlights or flashlights, and even in daylight, there were many things hidden in the trees, brush, and rocks. Humans depended upon their peripheral vision to protect them from danger. Even now you can detect movement much better with your peripheral vision than with your straight-ahead foveal vision! Our peripheral vision and hearing were literally essential tools for our survival and, even today, your healthy emotional survival depends to a great extent upon peripheral vision and hearing.

Peripheral vision has the impact it does on your emotions because of the way it affects your experience of foreground and background. Consider the difference between cartoon images and a painting or photograph of a landscape. Most cartoons are flat, two-dimensional images while landscapes are three-dimensional. Dimensionality conveys depth, that is, the phenomenon of foreground and background. In two-dimensional pictures, everything is on the same plane or linear surface, whereas in three-dimensional images, objects in the foreground are often larger and seem closer and more focused than objects in the background. There is a natural, congruent relationship between the objects of the foreground and background. It was not until the seventeenth century that landscape painting fully blossomed with the development of perspective as exemplified by the Dutch painter Jacob van Ruisdael's *The Burst of Sunlight*.

Remember as a child when you were taught to draw a road going through fields by starting at the bottom of the paper with a wide representation of the road and then making it narrower and narrower until it disappeared around a curve or into oblivion at the top of the picture. This way of representing a road or a river immediately gave the impression of depth, of a three-dimensional quality. If you put houses, animals, trees, or people in the drawing, the ones closest to the viewer are larger compared to a house or person midway back or on the edge of infinity. Imagine how incongruous it would look to have a horse in the foreground and another halfway into the background that was the same size or bigger. However, the object in the foreground is not so large that it becomes incongruous with the background objects.

Again, lift your eyes from this page you are reading and look at your surroundings. What is in the foreground of your vision, and what is in the background? Look out a window and notice the objects closest to you and those farthest away. The next time you're in a restaurant or eating with family or friends, look around you and pay attention to the difference between what you see in the foreground and in the background. All the things you see—objects and/or people—have a natural relationship between the foreground and background, and from this perspective they convey their relative size and distance from each other.

As I write this, I am sitting on my porch looking out through the screens that surround me. On the table in front of me, about five feet away, is a large amber candle. Beyond the table is a green lawn with an old, gnarled weeping willow. Behind that is a wall of darker, tall maples and elm trees. Bits of blue sky show through openings among the branches. The candle is in the foreground, the willow is in the background, and the maples and elms are in the far background. The candle is in normal proportion to the trees. It may appear large because I am closer to it than I am to the trees. However, the size of the candle stays congruent to the actual relative sizes and distances of everything I'm looking at. Imagine that you're having a conversation with a friend who is sitting at the opposite side of the couch you're sitting on. As you look at him, you can see the lamp on the table behind him and the books on the shelves lining that side of the room. You can see his face, his eyes and mouth, his body with his legs crossed. All the elements that you see are in a natural proportion to each other. His mouth isn't the size of his head or brightly lit compared to everything else, his head isn't out of proportion with his body, and his body isn't so large it blocks the lamp, table, and shelves. In other words, everything you're looking at has a normal relationship to each other; nothing is distorted. The natural proportional relationship between the foreground and background of what you're looking at depends not only upon actual size but the perceived relationship between size and distance as well as your position. Thus the candle I'm looking at seems bigger the closer I am to it, but at no time does it become so big that it blots out the willow behind it. There is a natural proportionality in my perception that tells me the candle is smaller than the willow and the willow is farther away from me than the candle. If you were to draw this picture, the candle would take up more space than the willow, and the willow would be drawn larger than the trees behind it. This gives the three-dimensional impression of depth but is proportional and relative to the actual size of the objects.

Peripheral vision and hearing are perceptual filters that govern how you perceive—rather than analyze, interpret, or judge—the information you are receiving through your eyes and ears. Your mind stores this information as images, sounds, and words. You also input information through your senses of smell, taste, and touch, but I am concentrating now on the visual and auditory senses. Your stored perceptions about the world do not represent the actual reality of what you have seen and heard, only your impression of that reality. Under normal circumstances, as you look at the trees, horses, and barn outside your window, you do not see the actual size of the barn that is farthest away from you, but you do see the proportional size in relationship to the horse closest to you and the fence that is even closer. If you were to go outside and stand very close to the barn, it would look a lot bigger than it does through your window. As you look at this scene, you know that the barn is much bigger than it appears because of the actual proportional relationships among the objects you're looking at.

Sometimes this normal relationship of foreground and background becomes distorted in your perception, and an object in the foreground becomes abnormally large or bright or focused contrary to reality. This is called tunnel vision. It can happen, for example, when you focus with so much intensity on someone's eyes that her eyes seem to fill her face, or when someone who is a few inches taller than you appears in your perception to tower over you.

When you were 12 years old and you brought home a report card with all As and Bs except for one D, that D seemed to jump off the paper. It seemed so much larger and clearer than the other marks! Of course, in reality, it wasn't. When you're trying to stop smoking and your friend takes out a pack of cigarettes and lights one, that pack of cigarettes seems to get larger and larger until it covers the entire table!

Tunnel vision is the visual distortion of something in the fore-ground of your experience as compared to the background. It results in loss of boundaries, causing you to merge with what-ever or whomever you're interacting. It could be your lover, your mother or son, or a brownie. It can happen with a boss who is criticizing you. You begin to lose your peripheral vision and hear-ing and focus on his face, primarily his mouth, from which comes words like "you didn't," "you should have," and "disappointed in you." You start merging with the negative words and emotions. You become the negativity. And you sure can't think constructively in that state.

"When I remember that experience now, Tommy and my father are just their normal size," Angela told me as we finished a session. She had been working on her lack of self-confidence around men. This was a woman in her mid-forties, a successful musician and widowed with two teenage children. The issue was very specific: whenever she wanted to assert herself with men, her sons, col-leagues, bosses, or friends, she became very nervous and found herself placating them. That in turn made her angry, and then she became belligerent. Angela felt bad about this behavior and how it sabotaged her self-confidence. She didn't want to fight. She wanted to stand up for her opinions, desires, and beliefs in a calm, centered way. We discovered that when she was between 5 and 10 years old, her father and older brother Tommy teased her when she expressed something she thought was important. She got very serious and dramatic when expressing herself, but her father and brother thought that was "cute" and laughed at her. We went back to one of the earliest of these memories, but this time I coached her to keep her boundaries by staying connected to her body, doing peripheral vision, and noticing how the memory was the same and different this time. We did this with several examples of the memories of her father and brother. With boundaries, the biggest difference she noticed in the memories was that her father and brother no longer appeared to tower over her. She saw them as their normal size. When these events actually happened, Angela was too young to maintain her boundaries in the face of the teasing she experienced. The scene became distorted and she developed tunnel vision. Her father and brother became, in her mind, much larger than life, filling her entire visual field. She lost her boundaries and merged with the teasing. As a result, she felt small, of no consequence, and not taken seriously. Perception is our subjective reality. Even with distortion, you experience what you perceive as the truth and never question it.

Angela's response to men in the context of ideas and serious conversation became generalized. Anytime she wanted to express an important idea to a man, she unconsciously saw the man as much larger than her and responded with anxiety and then anger. She could now see her father and brother (who was only four years older and three inches taller than her) as part of a larger picture in which their relative sizes were normal rather than looming over her. She began to understand that they had not teased her to be mean or to discount her ideas but because her serious demeanor amused them and made them laugh. She also recognized that they were being insensitive to her feelings but that that was their problem and not because something was wrong with her.

This type of distortion is common. Painful experiences in childhood leave a distorted perception in our memory. As children, we do not have stable boundaries, so tunnel vision occurs easily, resulting in loss of boundaries. A certain person in the memory becomes unnaturally large or close, and this becomes generalized to others in our present-day life. While we're aware of the resulting emotions and behavior, the distorted perception remains unconscious. When boundaries are created, the perceptual distortion is corrected, and we have the opportunity to make better decisions about who we are, what we're capable of, and what the world is.

Joe claimed that every time someone disagreed with him, he experienced a rush of adrenaline and wanted to physically attack the person. Sometimes he was able to restrain himself, but still his teeth and hands would clench, his breathing became rapid, and the skin on his face and neck became flushed. He got into a lot of physical fights. He frightened other people, and his friends and family considered him to be violent. He never seriously hurt anyone but walked a very fine line and managed never to be arrested. During the first five years of elementary school, Joe was constantly harassed by several of the school bullies. He never told his father, because his father was also somewhat of a bully and would have yelled at him to fight back and not be a wimp. The bullying was unknown to the teachers and adults, and he didn't tell anyone for fear that they would react like his father. This situation persisted until the fifth grade when Joe found a boxing class and a teacher he could trust and respect. He became a skilled boxer and began to fight back. As soon as he did, the bullies melted back into the darkness of their cowardice, but the damage had been done to Joe. He carried the wounds into adulthood, and they almost ruined his life.

We painstakingly went back to those early experiences and redid them with boundaries. At the time of this bullying, Joe was so young and the external circumstances were so frightening that it was impossible to maintain his boundaries. I guided Joe to act "As If" (pretend) he could have had boundaries back then and notice what difference having boundaries would have made in each situation. He discovered that with boundaries, he would have told some adults, even his father, about the bullying and would have asked for help in confronting these bullies. He realized he was not totally alone as he had always thought; there were other people around that he could have walked with and gotten some help from. Most importantly, he became aware that the bullies weren't bigger than him, there were just a lot of them. He was 8 years old and had lost his boundaries, and having tunnel vision had made the kids appear to be much bigger than him. They filled his entire visual field and seemed to be looming over him; nothing else existed but these huge menacing figures. For the next 20 years, on an unconscious level anyone who confronted him or even disagreed with him, appeared large and threatening. Today, at age 28, he was still experiencing those people as huge, looming, and menacing, blocking out everything else in the experience.

When Joe learned to apply peripheral vision to those memories, he disconnected the habitual association (someone disagrees with him and he experiences tunnel vision), which enabled him to maintain his boundaries. He is now able to actually see and hear the person who is disagreeing with him, to really listen to him, to stay aware of the other people in the scene, and to think about what he is saying. By maintaining his boundaries, Joe short-circuited the old, learned reaction and developed more choice about how he could respond. He still has a bit of a temper, but he can think now instead of just react. Disagreement no longer triggers the impulse to fight but rather to listen, think, and consider an appropriate response.

A woman in one of my classes, Kachina, reported an incident with her 12-year-old daughter that was unusual and troubling. It seemed to her to be an example of losing boundaries, but she couldn't explain how or why it had happened.

Kachina was a vegetarian who was married with one daughter. They were close to one another and had a happy and satisfying family life. Since Kachina was a vegetarian, they had had an agreement for many years that they would eat vegetarian meals in the home, but when they ate outside the home, each would eat whatever she wanted. One night, Kachina and her daughter ate dinner out, and as Kachina watched her daughter eat a hamburger, she became overwhelmed with feelings of being betrayed and disrespected. Kachina did not understand these feelings, since her relationship with her daughter was very positive, and she had long ago accepted the idea of her daughter eating meat when dining out. She had never felt this way before. I asked her if she had had dinner out with her husband during the same week that this surprising situation occurred with her daughter. She had, and it had been very pleasant. He had eaten a steak!

Struck by the similarity of both experiences and the distinct difference in Kachina's responses, I was curious about what was the difference that made the difference. Both events took place in a restaurant with a member of her family who had eaten meat. In one instance, Kachina felt upset and angry, and in the other she felt fine. I asked her to compare the two situations by picturing both in her mind and noticing any differences in her perceptions between the two. The emphasis was on how she saw and heard the two situations in her mind (how she felt in them was abundantly clear). Since I know that thought precedes an emotion, I wondered how she perceived these experiences. This is how she described them: "With my husband, I can see and hear him sitting across the table from me; I notice the window behind him and the view from it, and I can see some of the other tables and people eating around us. I can hear the low murmur of other conversations, the clink of silverware, and the music in the background. I'm aware of the color of the shirt he's wearing and the pattern and color of the tablecloth, the way the light reflects off the glasses, and the daisy in the small green vase in the middle of the table. I see his hands holding the knife and fork and moving as he eats. There is a soft pool of light coming from the lamp on the table, and I can see other areas of light and shadow on the other tables around us."

She continued, "When I had dinner out with my daughter, I can see her face, but mostly what I'm aware of is her mouth. Her mouth seems very large as though it's filling my entire vision. Everything around us is dark and far away. I can't see the table between us. I don't even see the rest of her body, only her face and especially her mouth. I can't see what's behind her or around us, only her mouth, her lips moving and the whiteness of her teeth chewing and chewing a very red, bloody hamburger. I don't hear anything either except her chewing and some words coming from her mouth in-between the bites."

This was clearly a case of extreme tunnel vision. I asked Kachina to think again of that dinner with her daughter, but instead of seeing only her daughter's mouth chewing, I asked her to deliberately and consciously see and hear her daughter in the memory in the same way she had seen her husband. It was obvious that with her husband she had both peripheral vision and hearing. I coached her to see her daughter's face and body in proportion to each other and the restaurant behind her, the table, silverware, and plates, the color of the tablecloth between them, the lights and people around them, and to hear the background sounds of the voices and music. Once Kachina had represented the memory in this way, her expression changed. I saw fewer frown lines, and her facial muscles relaxed, and she told me that she felt much better about the whole experience.

I asked Kachina to test her new perception. I suggested that she go out to dinner with her daughter, and when she ordered and ate her hamburger, to consciously focus on peripheral vision and hearing and to be aware of the colors, shapes, and sounds around her. The following week, Kachina reported that she had gone out to dinner with her daughter, who had ordered a hamburger. When Kachina began to get upset again, she remembered to stay aware of what was around her. She consciously maintained her peripheral vision, and her feelings remained calm and centered. She was able to enjoy the company of her daughter as she chewed her hamburger!

You might wonder why Kachina had tunnel vision and lost her boundaries with her daughter. There are many possible answers. Perhaps Kachina sensed that her daughter was moving into teen-age independence and felt a sense of separation that she wasn't quite ready for. Whatever the reasons, what was most important was that she found the tools to maintain her boundaries, thereby staying separate from and connected to her daughter. Sometimes the "how" is more important than the "why."

As with most things, the more you practice peripheral seeing and hearing consciously, the better you get. Practice may not produce perfection, but it can make your skills automatic. You climb the learning ladder. On the first rung, you are unconsciously incompe-tent—you don't even know what you don't know. On the second rung, you are consciously incompetent—you become aware of what you don't know. On the third rung, you become consciously competent—you are aware of what you know. Finally, on the fourth rung, you are unconsciously competent—your knowledge and skills are installed in your unconscious and have become automatic.

Here are a few ways to practice peripheral vision:

1. This is the same exercise that was described at the beginning of this chapter. While focusing on a spot in front of you, put your hands at ear height, about two to three feet away from your head, and wiggle your fingers; I'll call this the peripheral vision position. Play with the position of your fingers—move them forward and back until you've stretched your peripheral vision to the edge. Be aware of all you can see without actually looking directly at it. Do this for about 30 seconds every day for several weeks, and it will increase your awareness of your peripheral vision.

2.   Sit someplace quiet where you can be alone and undisturbed. Focus on a small spot in front of you, and describe in sensory detail, out loud, what you can see and hear around you without looking away from that spot. Do this several times a week.

3.   Before a meeting or encounter with someone with whom you have a tendency to "lose" yourself, have difficulty speaking up, or feeling the way you want to feel, do a practice session! Imagine the scene. See the other person, and run through an imaginary scenario of the encounter while putting your hands in the peripheral vision position. Wiggle your fingers and, as you go through your rehearsal of the future event, concentrate on the person you'll be talking to while maintaining awareness of the things around you without actually looking at them. Do this several times before the actual interaction.

Someone once complained to me about the effect he was having when doing peripheral seeing. He told me that when he was interacting with a client and paid attention to his peripheral vision, he felt distracted and unable to give the client his undivided attention and energy. It turned out that he had misunderstood peripheral seeing to mean giving equal attention to everything in his panoramic view. Not at all! You direct most of your attention and energy toward whatever your main focus is: the other person or object in the foreground of your experience. Your energy is totally centered on the other though you never lose awareness of what is in your peripheral vision. It's as though you're holding a beam of light with the most intense brightness on your subject of interest, with the outer edges of the light dimmer but still lighting the entire scene around you. Peripheral vision does not mean dividing your panoramic horizon into equal areas of attention!

Peripheral seeing and hearing help to create and maintain boundaries, whereas the loss of boundaries (tunnel vision/hearing) creates "a crumbly mess." Peripheral seeing and hearing are not connected to the creation of walls. Walls are created when you chronically see yourself or hear yourself either in the present situation or in your memories. It can be very useful to see and hear yourself as you develop an Observer Self (see Chapter 5). However, having no choice about this type of perception will result in excessive separation with little possibility of connection. Imagining a transparent acrylic glass wall between you and the rest of the world, and seeing objects and people as though they're far away, will also create walls. This holds true for external experiences and internal memories. In memories, you can increase the intensity of walls by making your images black and white and two-dimensional. Walls can be beneficial when there is a need to protect yourself, to give yourself some space, or to change your perspective, but without awareness of what you're doing and the choice to change it, it can create a prison in which you're isolated from the world. How you perceive your external and internal worlds determines your reality and your response to that reality.

The Rule of Three is a powerful metaphor, as the number three seems to convey a special magic. In the marketing field, they say that people have to see and/or hear of your product three times before they will buy it. In everyday life, a three-legged stool is the strongest and sturdiest. Three ways of doing something or getting somewhere means you have true choice—one way, you're stuck; two ways, you're on the horns of a dilemma; three ways, you have choice. Generally, you can take three points of view: your own, the other's, and that of the Observer Self. Gregory Bateson (1904–1980) was an American anthropologist, thinker, and author, and an important element of his thinking had to do with the concept of triple description, or how your subjective reality can be altered when you can describe the same experience three different ways. If you can fix a flat tire three different ways, I'll bet you never worry about getting one!

To "do" boundaries consciously and with choice, you must be aware of and proficient at the three skills of boundaries: the cognitive filter of simultaneous thinking, or noticing sameness and difference; the physiological filter of connecting to your body; and the perceptual filter of peripheral seeing and hearing. You know how to perform these skills. What's important is to become more aware of when you do them, when you don't, and what you do instead, and to practice them consciously in order to become unconsciously competent. You can then choose when you want to be separate, when you want to merge, or when you want to be separate *and* connected.

Once upon a time, there was a woman named Hannah who lived in Jerusalem. Hannah had a very serious problem: she was phobic that there were men under her bed. Every time she got into her bed, she became paranoid that there might be a man under it. The more she looked under her bed to check, the more anxious she became, even though each time she looked, the space was empty. As time went on, these anxiety attacks became panic attacks.

Finally Hannah went to see a psychiatrist who specialized in anxiety, phobias, and panic attacks. She was comforted by these weekly visits but still terrified that there might be a man under her bed. When she ran out of money, she could no longer afford to see the psychiatrist who, although fond of her and worried about her welfare, could not afford to work for nothing—he had a family to support.

Three months later, the psychiatrist was walking in the city and saw Hannah on the other side of the street. He crossed the street and greeted her. She looked better than he had ever remembered her looking. "How are you?" he asked. She answered, "Better than I've been in years!" The psychiatrist was curious and asked her about the problem they had been working on. "Oh, that's completely gone—no more. I'm free of it at last!"

Now the psychiatrist was *really* curious. How was it possible that he had seen her for three years with no improvement and here she was cured after three months of not seeing him? "How did this happen? What did you do?" he asked her. Hannah told him, "After I couldn't afford to see you anymore, I was desperate. I had to talk to someone, so I went to see my rabbi. I told him how panicked I got because I kept imagining there was a man under my bed. He told me to go to the hardware store, buy a saw, and go home and cut the legs off of my bed! I did—and now I'm fine."

Chapter VII

Boundaries and Relationships

This is an extended discussion of the many effects of boundaries, no boundaries, and walls on our most important relationships: parents and children, therapist and client, teacher and students, lovers, siblings, friends, business colleagues, employer and employees. Many ordinary problems are looked at through the lens of boundaries and the distortion of boundaries, suggesting a different approach to resolving these problems. Included are many personal examples in each of these areas designed to clarify the material previously covered and increase understanding and awareness.

The effects that boundaries, the lack of boundaries, or walls have on every type of relationship are profound. Boundaries make the difference between a successful or a broken relationship, between enlightenment and stagnation, between satisfaction and despair, between a wasted life and a productive one, between compassion and cruelty. Boundaries are the most basic and fundamental element of any functioning relationship. Let us now explore this.

The root of the word relationship is the verb "to relate." Relationships are about an ongoing, dynamic, ever-changing process, involving two or more people. And sometimes it is so hard, this relating. When you keep trying to balance your needs and wants and what you think the needs and wants of the other person are, you often make things more difficult. Harmonizing the multitudes of needs and wants would be more productive. Your need for approval and love drives you to want to please the other, but then you get scared or angry and pull back and retreat into yourself. Who's more important at this moment, you or the other? Whose wants are more important? As relationships become more intimate, there are fewer rules and less structure.

If you're a teacher or therapist, as I am, it's much easier to manage your relationships with your students and clients. This type of relationship is structured by certain rules and also by time: the length of the class or seminar, the length of the session. Within that frame, the rules are pretty clear. The clients' or students' needs take priority, and you are there to facilitate their learning or healing. You must have your boundaries in place, and you must be separate and connected. Even when your client is suffering, you cannot merge with her even though her pain reminds you of your own, nor can you put up walls to protect yourself from the other's overwhelming emotions. To merge with her would be to cheat her of your expertise, your knowledge, and your unique point of view. To isolate yourself behind walls would deprive her of your energy and your heart.

Within the frame of therapy and teaching, the issues of transference and countertransference are unavoidable and important issues. They are opportunities for growth and healing when your boundaries are maintained. As the client identifies with you, the therapist, and actually projects onto you the role of his mother, father, or significant other, he loses his boundaries with you. This is transference, and it has the potential of being very helpful in the progression of therapy as the client resolves his problems and begins to achieve his goals. While recognizing his loss of boundaries, you as therapist must continue to maintain your own, not taking it personally when he criticizes your responses to him or begins to come late to sessions. You still have the right to get irritated or annoyed by his actions and to express these feelings. When you have boundaries, you are separate enough to understand his projections onto you and yet connected enough to have a normal human response. This is the point of learning through transference: the client has an impact on the therapist, the therapist responds in a congruent way without stifling all response (walls) or overreacting (loss of boundaries). The client learns the honest, real consequences of his behavior and that the therapist—a person imbued with a significant historical meaning for the client—can respond to him with annoyance and still have a strong positive regard for him. You can get angry or disappointed with a person and still respect him, care for him, and love him. This is using the client's transference (loss of boundaries) to demonstrate what happens in real-life situations when you have boundaries.The client has an immediate experience of the effects of boundaries.

By maintaining boundaries, a therapist, is free to be authentic, to be real! Being separate and connected, you keep the bounds of professionalism and can respond as the unique human being you are. When therapists become extremely analytical and detached, you might call this being professional, but what's happening is they are isolating themselves behind walls. On the other hand, when you become too involved with your clients, forgetting that this is a job, you jeopardize appropriate separation. For therapists who are naturally empathetic, it is very easy for you to establish rapport with clients. You often unconsciously match your client's posture and breathing, and while this is an excellent rapport-building skill, if you're not aware that you're doing it, it can lead to merging and loss of boundaries. You are more prone to notice how you are similar to your client, and it is much more difficult to stay connected to your body. If you are an unconscious empathizer, you tend to merge with your clients and take on their feelings without realizing what is happening. How draining it can be when day after day you go home with all those anxious, depressed feelings and don't realize that they're not yours!

Countertransference occurs when the therapist's own feelings or issues get triggered by the client. Perhaps the therapist has unresolved issues with anger. You're not comfortable with conflict and avoid others' anger, and your client has trouble controlling her anger. When she demonstrates this, you want to tell her how inappropriate her anger is and how much more useful it would be to think before responding. Your suggestions are sound, but if they're coming from your own fear, you're sending a mixed message. She's triggering a response in you that is not a direct, clean response to what is happening in the present. Rather, it is a response to your past, your historical personal issues. Countertransference can be a useful tool for the therapist; you have, after all, an inside track on the issue. You can understand the feelings and give the therapeutic process the benefit of your struggles, insights, and possible solutions but only when you recognize that the feelings and responses you're having are your own issues being triggered by your client. You can only do this when you are separate and connected to your client.

When I was training and supervising therapists who were becoming overwhelmed by their client's feelings or taking something personally, I would remind them to hold onto the arms of their chair, feel their feet on the floor, and repeat to themselves, "This is my body over here in this chair." I would tell them to concentrate on their peripheral vision and ask themselves, "What does this remind me of in my own life? What is this similar to, and how is it different from that?"

I always tell young therapists starting out that whatever issue they have, they can be sure that clients with the same issues will find them. As you resolve one set of issues, others develop—and sure enough, clients with those issues will show up in your office. I noticed that whenever there was a predominant theme in the type of problems a therapist was treating, you could be sure that the therapist was also personally dealing with that particular issue in some way. I used to say, "The universe provides;" meaning that the clients with the same challenges that you are facing always seem to find you. This becomes an opportunity to guide you on the road of your personal evolution. As long as you are aware of and practice the skills of doing boundaries you'll not get stuck in any of the ditches of transference or countertransference — at least not for too long — and you will continue traveling.

Transference and countertransference are not bad or to be avoided. They occur in all kinds of therapy and counseling. Traditionally, these two words are more often associated with psychoanalysis than with other approaches to therapy. However, as long as you and your client are living beings with feelings, thoughts, and energy, you have an impact upon each other, which triggers all sorts of interesting responses. With awareness and boundaries, transference and countertransference are opportunities for personal evolution for both client and therapist.

Similar to and different from the therapist/client relationship is the relationship between teacher and student. In these relationships (as in the therapist/client relationship) the responsibility for maintaining boundaries is the teacher's.

The teacher who has walls isolates himself from any real human contact with his students, treating them as objects into which he is supposed to pour information. Indeed, a wall in any category (Causality, Mode, Threshold, and so on) will limit a teacher's effectiveness and blight his students' experience of learning. A teacher who does not connect his students' responses to his teaching might just as well send them their assignments via e-mail and return their grades to them at the end of the semester with no interaction or feedback.

> Stanley taught Introduction to Biology for 20 years, and he knew his material. He was comfortable with his knowledge and knew that he knew the subject matter. Even when he changed schools from a middle-class, suburban area to an inner-city, urban setting, he used the same lesson plan that he started with 20 years ago, using the same examples and telling the same stories. He delivered his lectures in a monotone and barely looked at his students—after all, he knew his stuff! For him, there was no connection between his behavior—his teaching—and the consequences—his students' responses. There was a wall between the two. Imagine how many of his students found themselves interested in biology or science in general!

Then there is the teacher who loses boundaries with her students. This can mean getting overly involved in their personal lives, spending hours trying to solve their problems, tutoring them endlessly, or even developing an inappropriate relationship with one of them. These behaviors will result in loss of perspective and judgment, working 12 hours each day to the detriment of the teacher's private life, burn-out, and ultimately bad feelings between teacher and students because of unrealistic and unfulfilled expectations.

It's important for a teacher to be involved with her students, to care about them, and to respond to their needs and interests, but in an appropriate way, both for the students' and the teacher's benefit. Boundaries provide the foundation for this type of challenging relationship.

Specific time frames that structure interactions such as teaching, therapy, interviews, or meetings make it is easier to maintain boundaries, because these interactions are distinct and separated from the rest of life by certain time constraints. Structured time frames create a specific context in which you know what "hat" you should be wearing.

What about relationships in which there is no specified time frame? Rather, the time is *always*. Parent–child relationships are a good example. Since children don't have sophisticated and stable boundaries, they tend to merge with their parents, identifying with the parents' feelings, thoughts, and values. Young children are extremely connected to their parents and lack a sense of separation and individuality. In fact, separation frightens them because their identity is within the parents and not within themselves. If they feel separated, they may experience themselves as not existing, as nothing—and this is terrifying. In adolescence, children begin to bond and merge with their friends and to place their identity within their social environment. The walls that go up between children and parents at this time are actually positive. They allow the child some space within which to experience himself and begin the exploration of who he is, separate from his parents. It is a normal psychological development called individuation. Of course, at least in a functioning family, the wall is not total nor present all the time. More likely, the child bounces back and forth between putting up walls and having no boundaries. If the connection with the parents and their influence remains strong, the young person does not merge completely with friends and the preteen and teenage culture.

It is a difficult period. As a parent, you may ask, "How do I maintain my authority?" "How do I respond to what feels like total rejection?" "How do I handle this constant rebellion?" First of all, rejoice in the fact that they are rebelling. Would you want them not to separate from you, never becoming the separate, unique individuals they were meant to be? Go 15 or 20 years into the future: how would you like to have a dependent, compliant, and merged son or daughter now? A parent is merely the vehicle through which a human being enters this world. She or he is the caretaker who nourishes the child until he can create his own life. As a parent, you are the center of your young children's life, but as he gets older you move more and more to the edges until he is the center of his life and in due course his own child's life. So the cycle continues. This is not to say that you are not deeply loved by and very important to your children, but the center of energy inevitably changes. For some parents this is an extremely difficult and painful transition. Boundaries will help!

Appreciating that your daughter's apparent rejection of you and your values is a healthy and positive thing for her will create a more solid foundation for your relationship. From this perspective, you can practice the skills of boundaries. Rehearse them in imagined conversations with her. I know the first response to her rejection is to feel hurt and to want to put up walls to protect yourself. The danger is that you will bounce between walls and no boundaries, especially when she needs you. Imagine if she comes to you for solace after a fight with a friend or a breakup with a boyfriend, and you respond to her merging with you with your own loss of boundaries. Now you're merged with each other: feeling each other's love and pain and becoming one. This feels as good as when she was 2 years old. However, two days later, she's made up with her friend or met another boy and she "ditches" you—and the walls go back up! Now you're devastated or angry. So you put up a wall, and now there's very little real communication—it's hard to contact each other through a brick wall. Sometimes a father gets so hurt or disappointed that his son is not living up to the values and ideals that are most important to him that he puts up an impenetrable wall that is never breached. Children and young adults don't know how to break down a parent's wall. They feel rejected and not loved for who they are instead of who they're *expected* to be—the son or daughter of the parents' dreams. This is so sad, because I believe most of the time there is love between the parent and child but neither knows how to connect after the years have cemented the walls between them.

It is up to the parent to be the adult and take responsibility for maintaining boundaries. Ask yourself if your hurt, your disappointment, or anger is there because you've merged your hopes and unrealized dreams for your life with your child's life. Have you projected your desires or fears for your child onto him? Is your pain at the prospect of "losing your baby," giving up the adult–child relationship for an adult–adult relationship, about your own lack of identity? Your own lack of a life that is separate *and* connected? If you answer yes to any one of these questions,

97

then you must attend to your own issues and begin to create your life as you want it to be. If you answer no, then consciously and purposefully practice boundaries with your child. It is natural to grieve the loss of the baby, the child in your life, but do not give in to the temptation to hold onto that. The rewards of an adult–adult relationship with your son or daughter are great—and this is as it should be.

Even when you get through this period of separation, don't think your challenges with boundaries and your children are over! I have a 30-year-old son. One day, we were talking in my living room, and he was upset about his financial situation. He couldn't pay all of his bills that month, and he couldn't go away with his friend because he didn't have enough money. He was very bummed out, and his emotions were leaking out all over the place. I had felt fine before he came to visit, but I was starting to feel agitated and negative. Recognizing what was happening, I told myself, "I'm not my son; I'm sitting on the couch and he is sitting in the chair opposite. He and I are separate human beings; he's over there and I'm here." I began to imagine the emotion that was coming off him as a circle of energy around him, and I had my own circle of energy around me. The two circles were different colors, and the energy was pulsing around us in separate streams. Sometimes the edges of the circles touched, but the flows do not mix; they stayed separate. This image really helped me to keep my perspective. I cannot solve his problems for him. I cannot make him happy! The trouble is that for all parents, once upon a time we *could* solve our children's problems, and we *could* make them happy. We could take the splinter out of his foot and make the pain go away, or teach him how to catch a ball so that he could play with his friends, or tell him a bedtime story, or take him to a movie, or buy him a matchbox car—and make him happy. Not anymore! Only *he* can solve his problems and make himself happy. You can empathize, sympathize, listen, and offer encouragement and support, but you can't do it for him. Because, as a mother or a father, you bonded with your newborn infant, you totally merged with this cosmic miracle, it is very easy to go back to the place of no boundaries. Be aware of this tendency. Sometimes it's okay to indulge yourself, but know when it is happening and what you're doing and then *choose* to "do" boundaries.

In the beginning of life with your child, the issue of boundaries is nonexistent; she is totally a part of you and you are one with her. As time goes by, the question of separation arises: the mother's and father's consideration of their life *separate* from their child. Then the child herself begins the process of separation and individuation, exploring her beingness, her uniqueness as a person. This is gradual, and the guidelines are not always clear or precise. The questions, "When do I have boundaries, and when do I merge with my daughter or my son?" are never fully and completely answered. I believe it is often enough to simply ask the question. The value of a question is not the answer or the information gathered as a result; it is where it sends you, where and how it directs your thinking. Questions direct your thinking like highway signs direct your trip! A really good question can change your direction and send you down a new path to brand new realizations and possibilities. A simple shift in language can also reinforce boundaries and profoundly impact a relationship. The use of "I" statements rather than "you" statements serves to make the distinction between you and the other. By making "I" statements such as, "I'm upset, I don't like that behavior, I feel disrespected by that, I worry when I don't hear from you, I feel angry when you ..." "I'm hurt when you do ..." You are owning your own feelings as distinct from your child's. You are saying, "We are different people and your actions affect me—I have my feelings." "You" statements tend to blame and judge. They sound like this: "You're being disrespectful, you don't care that I'm worrying about you, you're ignoring me, you never ..." and "You don't ..."

"I" statements reinforce being separate and connected. "You" statements mush the distinction between two people and trap the other into defensiveness.

Although children do not have the psychological maturity to maintain stable boundaries, you can begin when they are 6 months old or even earlier to verbally make the distinction between you and them. I think parents forget how perceptive children are, thinking that if you don't cry in front of them, they won't know you're sad, or if you're worried about paying the rent, you can keep this from them by not talking about it. I don't mean to say that you should burden your children with all your concerns, but boundaries and the expression of them can make a positive difference. For example:

> You're a single mother and a lawyer who has worked out a part-time schedule with your employer. You have a 15-month-old son, Brandon, who stays with his grandmother when you're working. It's a great set-up: your boss is very understanding about sudden inevitable minor crises, you're doing what you're good at, and you're making good money. One day, you hear through the office grapevine that the firm is not doing well financially, is in danger of going out of business, and may fire a number of lawyers. You know what that means: you'll be one of the first to go. That evening, you're at home with your baby; you're worried, distracted, and on edge. He seems to be particularly demanding tonight—and you lose it. You yell at him, he cries, and you feel guilty. This is the perfect time to make a distinction for him between you and him: "I'm sorry, Brandon. Mommy's worried about some things at work and I'm cranky. I'll work everything out but I'm just cranky and grumpy tonight. It's not you. Let's read a story together."

You've told him verbally that sometimes you feel irritated, sad, or upset and that these feelings are not about him. They are not his fault. He will not understand cognitively but he will emotionally, and it will help you get back on track. This distinction is important to make with your children. You're human, you're perfectly human, meaning that you're imperfect and make mistakes. Sometimes you take your feelings out on others or get impatient, or you're mean or unfair. Because children don't have stable boundaries, they blame themselves for your feelings unless you begin to make that distinction between them and you. When you tell them that you're cranky or feeling sad today, you're establishing that the two of you are separate and can have different feelings and that's okay. It is also important to remember your responsibilities as the parent. Your child is not your confidant, your nurturer, or your therapist. Keep your boundaries in place; *you* are the adult, *you* are the parent, and as such, you must not overwhelm your children with your problems. At the same time, you cannot pretend that nothing's wrong when you're depressed because your lover left you, or the new job didn't come through, or you're worried about some other difficulty in your life.

Secrets are one of the most destructive elements in any relationship, especially with children, because they always know what's going on at an emotional level. No matter how positive and noble your intentions are, keeping secrets in a family either by lying or not saying anything is like a deadly acid that slowly and steadily eats away at whatever it touches until nothing is left.

> I had a client whose father died when he was 2 years old. It happened unexpectedly; he remembered waking up in the middle of the night to strange sounds in the house: people going up and down the stairs, hushed voices, whispers, muffled crying. When he cried out, his aunt who lived with them came in and explained that everything was fine—some friends had come to visit for a few hours. He was told to go back to sleep. In the morning, he was told his mother and father went away on a trip for a few days. When his mother came back alone, she said his father was away on business and that she had a bad cold. And so this cover-up continued for another year when finally he was told his father had "gone to a happier place." The family's intention was to protect the 2-year-old from the shock and confusion of the loss of his father which, they reasoned, he couldn't understand. The problem was that he knew something terrible had happened. He knew something was going on but he was excluded. Not knowing why his father wasn't around yet knowing something bad was connected to this disappearance frightened and confused him, and he felt like he was somehow to blame. This experience deeply affected him, making him anxious that anyone he got close to might just suddenly disappear. As an adult, he had this vague but pervasive sense that bad things that happened around him were his fault, and it was hard for him to trust that other people were telling him the truth.

Whatever the difficulty or the disaster, it is always better to be honest with your children, but this does not mean putting the burden on them, using them as a receptacle for your emotions, or expecting them to make you feel better. You must keep your boundaries with your children—you are the adult and responsible for them. The *way* you tell them and how much detail you give them depends on their age but, above all, be honest. No matter how painful and upsetting it may be for them, they will ultimately feel safer. By being honest, you are creating a congruent environment: your actions, words, attitude, and emotions match the external situation. In this way, you're not giving your children mixed messages that make them confused and frightened.

Most of you have heard this advice about parenting: discipline the behavior, not the child. What this means, of course, is that you should distinguish between a child's behavior and the totality of her being, who she is. When 2-year-old Suzy looks at you with that devilish grin and spits her whole mouthful of pudding right at you, making a mess all over your clothes, you might be upset, especially when you're late for an important meeting. Keeping in your mind the boundary between your little darling's *behavior* and *who she is*, you have every right to express your upset at her behavior *not* her personhood. It's not okay to yell, "You're a bad girl!" It is okay to say, even loudly, "Spitting is *not* okay, and I don't like it." Then distract her with something that's fun for her and less destructive for you. The distinction between your daughter's behavior and who she is is fundamental to nurturing her self-esteem and self-confidence while teaching her what is acceptable, respectful behavior toward you and others. It sends the message clearly to her that you can be angry, upset, and hurt by her while continuing to love her.

In considering boundaries in the parent–child relationship, I have concentrated on the point of view of the parent. Let us now look at this from the point of view of the child, particularly in older children from the teenage years on. Even when you're 70, if you're lucky enough to have a living parent, you will always be that parent's child. It's useful in this relationship to be aware that your tendency as the child, of any age, is to bounce between having no boundaries, where you merge with your mother, expecting her somehow to make everything okay, or putting up a wall and detaching from her so you don't have to deal with her at all. It is very difficult to experience your parent as a human being separate from you. After all, you have no history of this: you were born and then merged appropriately with her. This was the foundation of your life. Now, you're expected to see her as a whole person, separate from you!—a person with her own thoughts, feelings, and opinions that have nothing to do with you. How could this be possible? You may never entirely experience it, but at least be aware that it is true. Your mother and your father were whole, separate people before you came along. The next time you see your parents, look at them with peripheral vision. See them as part of the panorama of the world, and see their relationship to that world rather than seeing them merely as your mother or your father and dwelling on what that means to you personally. You might feel that they're obstacles to your progress, so you ignore them and put up walls between you and them. You're isolating yourself, walling yourself off from your history and your heritage; you are in fact a mix of the two of them. From your point of view, it can be a very interesting and rewarding experience to resist that either/or of no boundaries or walls, of either blaming them for everything, expecting them to make your life all better, or pretending that they don't exist, or that they can never understand you. You are separate from your parents *and* you are connected. Honor both by "doing" boundaries with them, and you will discover who these imperfect people are and, by extension, a piece of who you are.

> Jenette and her mother have always been very close; they love and respect each other and consider each other their best friend. As her mother gets older, Jenette does not give any thought to her mother's mortality—she simply denies it and doesn't think about it. A few years ago, her mother got seriously sick and Jenette was very worried and scared. She was constantly at the hospital. After a week, when her mother was released and was recovering, Jenette switched gears. She put her head in the sand and put up walls. She pretended that her mother was fine and needed no help—and disappeared for a while. Jenette put up walls because once the immediate crisis was over, she couldn't deal with her mother's advancing age and possible decline. It was easier to block this out with walls. The problem was that her mother felt abandoned and felt she couldn't depend on Jenette except in extreme crisis or when everything was going smoothly. When she said how this hurt her, Jenette felt unappreciated and that whatever she did was not enough. Keeping your boundaries in this kind of situation is difficult because it means staying connected to your feelings. In this case, the feelings are fear, pain, and taking responsibility for your role in the relationship. Today, Jenette and her mother continue "doing" their boundaries and deepening their relationship.

There's a saying, "What goes around, comes around." Life is a circle, and sometimes the beginning and end are very similar. In the beginning of life, you are totally dependent on your parents, and sometimes in the end, your parents are dependent on you. Your roles become reversed. The beginnings and the ends are special times from which you can learn and evolve. You are starting and completing a circle, and with each completion comes fulfillment. This circle is a beautiful and special phenomenon in the universe of your life.

I love all the stages of my Irish Wolfhounds' lives, but there is something very special about the beginning and end. To me, Irish Wolfhound puppies are so loving, funny, adorable, curious and growing, growing, growing and learning, learning, learning. They're into everything, they trust totally, they give unconditional love, excitement of discovery, absolute joy in every greeting. And they are a tremendous amount of work, just like a newborn baby. It's a constant, 24-hour demand; there's no rest except when they sleep, and you never know when they'll wake up and start all over again on their exciting exploration of the world—with every orifice in full working order. When they're older and calmer, understanding and honoring the rules of life with you, they give back your love and companionship tenfold. And then suddenly they're old. A Wolfhound's life expectancy is between six and nine years, so this cycle happens rather rapidly. The old, veteran Wolfhound is much slower, wiser, and more tolerant. He loves to nap in the sun during the cold winter months and on the cool bare floor in the heat of the summer. They are your constant companions, always by your side without ever getting in the way—except when they lie in front of the sink as you're trying to wash the dishes! They still love to go for walks, though not as far as they used to; they get tired and depend on you to know when to turn back. Their back legs get weaker, and they have trouble getting up. Sometimes you have to help them, and getting into the car is very embarrassing. The veteran is very dignified and doesn't like the world to know about his accidents—his digestive track is not what it used to be. He allows you to lift his hind quarters into the car and clean up his accidents because he trusts you. He knows that you don't think less of him because of his infirmities. Some nights you don't get much sleep because he has to go out frequently, and then there are the trips to the vet. And when it is time for him to go to the rainbow bridge where he'll wait for you, if you're paying close attention, you'll know. His acceptance of the end means that you too have to accept it. Then you share the closing of the great hound's circle. You cry and mourn, and then continue, for there are other hounds that need you. But you never forget those you have known. Each one has marked your heart and your soul.

The relationship of lovers is probably the most dramatic of all relationships; not necessarily the most important but certainly the most dramatic and the most intense. You see in the other who you want to be or who you're afraid of being. Lovers meet with their hearts, minds, souls, and bodies; two individuals experiencing a unity of thinking, feeling, and being. It is glorious and incredible and dangerous. The "urge to merge" is compelling in everyone, and when you meet your lover, the temptation to lose yourself in the other is overwhelming. That is as it should be, but the question is, "For how long?" "When?" For lovers, the dance of together and apart, individual and merged, dependent and independent, setting boundaries and having no boundaries, is constant. It can shift many times in one day. It is like the shape of a cloud, continually changing and moving. Contrast this with the relationship of a parent and child, where you begin merged but gradually establish boundaries as the optimum state. With a lover, it is desirable to have boundaries and also to merge at times: when making love, when thinking as one, feeling as one, being as one in a psychic state of togetherness; when sharing intimate, painful, joyous memories that the other can feel as though she is you. Why not stay merged always? Because then you are no longer a whole person, an individual who learns and evolves. Without your individuality, the space to be separate, to be you, you would ultimately be less and less of who you are and you will feel frustrated, needy, and unfulfilled. Your lover will begin to feel suffocated, burdened by your dependency and the passion, romance, and true connection will disappear. Boundaries can be difficult for lovers because the greatest seduction of having a lover is the illusion that you are not alone. When someone else thinks like you do, feels your pain, and needs you, you can pretend that you are not really alone—you have your lover. This is a grand and comforting illusion, and it truly is an illusion—a self-deception!

You are alone from the moment the umbilical cord is severed and you are separate from your mother's womb until the day you die.

This is not a bad thing; it simply means that you are a unique being who is whole and complete in yourself. You can connect deeply and profoundly with others as you travel the road of life. You impact and are impacted by others; your contact with them nurtures and challenges you to realize your potential. But you *are* alone. This idea frightens many, and they grasp at love to save them from this fate of aloneness. When you become and stay one with the other, you either kill the very love that brought you together or you kill the *self* that is your essence. The dark side of the oneness of two people making love or communing with each other's soul is the loss of identity—when the oneness is compulsively held onto by one or both persons.

It is a cliché that two people who have been together for a long time finish each other's sentences and, like most clichés, this one is based on fact. The familiarity of long association creates a kind of intimacy. You know the other's habits and ways of thinking, opinions, and reactions, so you frequently assume that you know what he's feeling or thinking before he even says anything. Many times you're right, because you do know a lot about this person. Problems arise when you assume that you know your lover as well as you know yourself. You blur the distinctions between the two of you and lose sight of the fact that he is a separate individual with his own unique thoughts, feelings, identity, desires, fears, and dreams who needs the space of his individuality. When you lose your boundaries, you no longer really see him or hear him, and he might as well not even be there. The other becomes invisible. You're not really reacting to him but to who you *assume* he is. Your relationship is then with your own projection of your hopes, fears, and desires. This is not true intimacy. Intimacy is when two separate *whole* persons share their deepest thoughts and feelings, when they honor each other as individuals. They demonstrate this honor through attending to the other as unique, discovering the other rather than simply assuming knowledge. This relationship may become difficult in real time and life when habitual familiarity takes over. Being aware and sensitive to the natural inclination to assume that you know what's going on with the other in any long-term relationship will help you to avoid this trap.

Assuming that you know what the other is thinking or feeling without any concrete expression on his part is called mind reading or intuition. Intuition is a valuable ability but only when you're aware that you're using it and do not allow yourself to fall in love with your assumptions. You must realize that what you're assuming to be true is the product of your own experience, your own limited observations and habitual associations. You have an equal chance of being right or wrong. It's fine to "mind read" another, but check out your conclusions! Ask! Ask and be open to the possibility that you're actually wrong about what you're assuming. It's okay to be wrong! Being wrong or right is a momentary state of being that passes in the wink of an eye. When you're wrong, you can learn something for the next time, and when you're right, you can take action; but without awareness that your assumptions are coming from *your* model of the world, you're building communication on a house of cards.

The familiarity that comes from long and intimate association is the glue that holds a relationship together, but it can also cement two people into the trap of repetitious negative loops of thinking, feeling, and behavior. Most of the time, when couples fight and miscommunicate, they do so over small, unimportant issues. Their fights become habitual; repeated predictably over and over again.

Assumptions and mind reading make this possible. When these are positive they create an aura of understanding and intimacy; however when they're negative they create a loop of unending misunderstanding and resentment. When you mind read, you lose boundaries between yourself and the other. Since intuition depends on the momentary dissolving of boundaries, if this happens without awareness and continues over a prolonged period of time, you're building the foundation of disaster. Mind read all you want, develop your intuition *and* maintain your boundaries so that you never lose awareness that the other is a separate and different individual from you. Except, of course, when you choose to!

The ability to be intimate with someone is desired by most people. It is connection on the deepest level, with two people sharing their most personal and private natures, their angels and demons, their strengths and weaknesses. Being able to look into the other's soul and see who is really there rather than the projection of your hopes or fears, allowing the other to see all of you without the social masks, the defensive and protective personas, is the greatest gift. It is built on acceptance of self as *separate* and the courage to be vulnerable and to *connect*. Positive self-esteem is necessary for this to happen, and I will develop this theme in greater detail in Chapter 10.

People tend to love each other the way *they* want to be loved. If you feel loved when the other touches you, then you will touch your lover to convey *your* love. You may want to be told in words how the other feels about you; if so, that is how you will communicate *your* feelings. What if what makes your lover feel loved is different from what makes you feel loved? How's that going to work? Not very well, I think. This requires that you remember and act on the fact that no matter how intimate you and your lover are sometimes, you *are* separate beings with different needs and wants and different ways in which these are satisfied. You've got to accept being *separate* in order to discover what makes your partner feel loved. After all, when you love someone, you want that person to feel loved by you, even when it means acting or doing some things differently, engaging in actions that are unfamiliar or even unimportant—to *you*.

Jane feels loved when Bill touches her, so she touches Bill a lot. Bill feels loved when he's told so in words, so Bill tells Jane how he feels about her. And both feel dissatisfied, as though something were missing in their relationship!

> Here is Stephanie and Milton. Stephanie is a very loving and caring person who tends to lose boundaries with her significant others. Her intimate relationships are very, very important to her, and she is able to step inside the other—Milton—and feel his feelings. She then adjusts her behavior to take care of him and make him happy, because she "cannot" be happy until he is. She feels important because she has the ability to make Milton happy. Milton is a passionate and loving man who uses walls to protect himself from others' pain and neediness. He also needs to be by himself a good deal. Once he knows and trusts someone, he bounces from walls to no boundaries. There is great passion in the relationship between Stephanie and Milton. The problems arise when Milton needs to be alone. He needs this time alone as much as he needs air to breathe. He is not trying to get away from Stephanie; he just needs time and space by himself. Stephanie feels upset and rejected

by his behavior because she's having trouble accepting that he and she are separate. She thinks that she should be the one to satisfy all his needs. She mistakenly believes that he is all she needs to make her happy. This causes Milton to put up walls against Stephanie's hurt—and she feels more and more rejected. When Stephanie has boundaries, she'll be able to enjoy her separateness from Milton and feel secure in their mutual connection. She'll understand that needing his own space is part of who Milton is, not a reaction to her. Milton's ability to maintain boundaries rather than putting up walls when Stephanie feels hurt will mean that he can stay connected to her. He'll be able to communicate to her that getting alone-time is something important to him, and it does not mean that he is unhappy with her. He will stay open and available, which will reassure her and strengthen their connection. Boundaries will help Stephanie experience her strength in separation and Milton his freedom in connection.

Intimacy cannot exist without boundaries. Intimacy is the sharing of the deepest parts of one's self, and the presence of walls would make this impossible. On the other hand, without boundaries, you merge with what you think are the other's thoughts and feelings and expect the other to do the same. Intimacy requires recognition of the other and a willingness to open yourself to the other and to receive her vulnerability. What makes intimacy difficult for some people is a lack of understanding and awareness of boundaries and how to "do" them. Remember how language can impact boundaries—either reinforcing them or causing the loss of boundaries or walls. The use of "I" rather than "You" statements opens up communication between people and provides the space needed to hear and respond. When you're angry, hurt, or fearful in your relationship with your lover, make the effort to use "I" statements. You will be surprised and delighted by the impact that has on your communication.

Historical influence has a huge impact on your experience of an intimate relationship. If you grew up in a family where your mother had no boundaries and your father had walls, this is the model of togetherness that you learned. You learned that being feminine and nurturing meant losing yourself in the other; being masculine and strong meant no expression of emotions, maintaining a "stiff upper lip." This walled-off definition of gender and gender values is changing as people allow more permeability between values and experience. If you grew up in this environment, you have to create a new model of what an intimate relationship is. If as a child you were an extension (no boundaries) of your mother or father, and then as you got older you began to separate and express this separation by being "different" with your own values, emotions, and behaviors, your parents may have reacted as though you were annihilating them. You were one with them, and to deny this was to deny them existence. This dynamic can severely limit you in your intimate relationships as an adult. You will either make yourself an extension of your mate or expect him to be an extension of you. You will see his development as a separate person as a threat to your identity and to the relationship, and you will try to protect yourself and your individuality by withdrawing behind walls.

> Tim and Nancy grew up in the type of family just described. When they got together, Nancy was a timid, withdrawn student, and Tim was a rising star at his brokerage firm. After graduating from a prestigious art school and several years' experience as a graphic artist, Nancy became more confident and aware of herself as an individual. This threatened Tim, because he felt as though she was no longer the person with whom he fell in love. Nancy now disagreed with him about politics, status, and success! He felt betrayed, and he put up walls. He had considered her an extension of himself. At the beginning of their relationship, she had no clear sense of herself and allowed herself to be swallowed up by Tim's strength, confidence, and enthusiasm. As Nancy grew in her awareness of herself and her own potential, she began to feel as though she had to make a choice between the relationship with Tim and her development as a separate person. Because she had been so much a part of Tim, she felt that by changing, she would destroy their relationship. Tim felt as though Nancy's changing would destroy his very existence. Is there hope for this couple? What could happen if they stepped out of the fog of their family history that taught a model of togetherness based upon the female projecting her life onto the male and the male existing behind isolating walls? They could begin to see and hear each other as separate human beings who, contrary to what they learned as children, have the right to different opinions and desires and can still connect in a loving relationship.

Dora and Sophie have been together for five years and have decided to get married. Their families were extremely supportive and enthusiastic. Sophie had grown up in a family of several ministers, and a favorite uncle was going to preside over their wedding. They made elaborate plans, choosing a special place in the country where a natural cathedral of willows and grape arbors created the perfect ambiance. Sophie had always dreamed of getting married and creating an unforgettable experience. She had wanted this for several years and had waited patiently for Dora to join her in this dream. Dora loved Sophie very much and she loved the idea of a wedding and getting married. However, there were parts of Dora that didn't want the formal, legal structure of marriage. She was working herself up to do it because she knew how important it was to Sophie. She tried to convince herself that she wanted it as much as Sophie because she did want a life with Sophie and, if she didn't marry Sophie, how could they have a lasting relationship? Dora had gotten stuck in the trap of loss of boundaries through generalization. She was feeling as if marriage equaled her and Sophie's entire relationship. She was trying to wall off the parts of her that didn't want to get married and mind reading that their relationship would be damaged if they didn't marry.

I knew that those parts Dora was trying to deny would eventually come back and bite her in the behind. They would sabotage the relationship, something she desperately didn't want to do. I asked Dora and Sophie to ask themselves the following questions: "What will marriage do for us personally? What will getting married do for our relationship?" I reminded them that in any relationship there are three separate entities: each of the two people, and the relationship itself. Dora and Sophie are not the relationship, the relationship is not Dora and Sophie. Their interactions, as they relate to each other with feelings, thoughts, and behaviors, create a third entity: the relationship. Just as it is important for each human being to have boundaries to maintain her uniqueness and integrity and to connect to the world around her, it is also critical that a relationship have boundaries. In order to distinguish it from the background of many other experiences, new information—thoughts, emotions, and sensations—will permeate the relationship and constantly shape it. A relationship is a dynamic process that will live only when it continues to grow and change as circumstances affect it, while remaining constant and stable at its core.

Dora and Sophie decided not to get married with the traditional rituals and legal structure. Instead, they created their own ritual that allowed them to celebrate with friends and family and publicly pledge their commitment to each other. This made both of them happy and was a congruent expression of their very special relationship.

Boundaries are also a vital component of friendships. Some friendships are very intimate without the sexual component, and some are structured around a shared passion or avocation, social events, hobbies, causes, or random circumstances. Whatever the catalyst may be for the beginning of a friendship, the friendship is nurtured by mutual interests and appreciation. The dilemma of a friendship is in the nature of this very personal connection: when to take things personally and when not to.

Two young men, William and Bobby, have been friends for several years. William is a volunteer fireman and a member of his community's Fire Department, and he convinced Bobby to become a member. The department keeps track of how many calls each member responds to. At the end of each year, awards were given based in some measure on this number. Bobby became an enthusiastic member responding to a lot of calls, and he bragged to William about it. He was younger than William and had usually been in his shadow. William started to take Bobby's competitiveness personally, feeling as if Bobby was not respecting him or the friendship. William was devoted to the department and derived great personal satisfaction from helping others and his community. Bobby's competitive behavior started to overshadow their entire relationship, as William assumed that Bobby was acting this way to show him up. William was finding his identity as a volunteer fireman, and this made him vulnerable to taking Bobby's behavior personally. Boundaries were lost on William's part in three categories: **Generalization** (part equals whole; Bobby's competitiveness equaled lack of respect for their entire friendship, **Mode** (mind reading; William assumed that he knew what motivated Bobby's behavior), and **Identity** (I am). William was beginning to have no sense of self separate from his position as a volunteer fireman. When William realized what he was doing and regained his boundaries, he was able to separate himself from Bobby's behavior and allow Bobby the space to do his thing without taking it personally. Their friendship survived and actually strengthened. With his boundaries back in place, William was able to talk to Bobby about what he was doing without anger or resentment. Bobby heard him out and recognized some of his own issues. They were able to listen to each other without letting destructive assumptions and loss of boundaries block their communication.

When is it appropriate to take what the other person says or does personally, and when does taking it personally reflect your own loss of boundaries? Being affected personally by your friend is what friendship is all about. When the result is positive, it reaffirms your relationship. When it is negative, there's a question to be answered: is it due to your loss of boundaries, or is it a violation of your values? This question involves threshold: your values regarding friendship—your emotional, cognitive, and behavioral experience of friendship. When boundaries distinguish this experience from other experiences, the threshold becomes dynamic and stable. When there are no boundaries there is no distinct and personal experience of value, and walls make the value rigid and inflexible. You know when a friendship is worth keeping or when it should be let go: your values are either satisfied or violated. However, in order for this threshold to be useful and beneficial, you must have a strong unique experience of what is important to you in friendship *and* this experience must be connected to changing circumstances. In other words, your threshold for friendship, or indeed for anything important to you, must be both stable *and* flexible.

When you find yourself taking something personally *and* it's painful, ask yourself these questions: "Is it appropriate for me to feel hurt? Has my friend violated an important value? Is that value reasonable in these circumstances? Or have I lost my boundaries with my friend and taken something personally that really has nothing to do with me? Is this my friend's issue, not mine?"

Cassie once had a friend named Penelope, and then suddenly she didn't have Penelope as a friend any more. They became close friends during their mutual involvement in a creative project. They shared many interests and values, but there were some significant differences between them, which seemed to add to the spice of their relationship. Penelope lived in the suburbs of the city, while Cassie lived in the center of the city. Penelope came into the city often for meetings with her agent and publisher, and so meeting in the city became the norm. They did several projects together, but as time went by, Penelope seemed to resent that she was always the one who came to Cassie's neighborhood. Cassie was single, ran a business, and had several children at home while Penelope was an artist. She had a husband, but her children were grown and gone. Cassie kept putting off traveling to the suburbs in order to see her friend. One afternoon before they were scheduled to have dinner, Cassie got a disturbing call and learned that an old colleague was threatening to sue her. She was very upset and became absorbed by this problem, making many phone calls to other colleagues and lawyers. She finally got home around 8:00 p.m. and was trying to escape worrying about the situation by watching the evening news when she suddenly remembered her 7:00 p.m. dinner date with Penelope. It was 8:45 p.m.! She rushed out of her house and to the restaurant where they had agreed to meet. Penelope was not there. Cassie ran home and called Penelope's home. Her husband answered, and he said that Penelope was not home yet. Cassie explained to him what had happened, apologized several times, and asked that Penelope call her when she got home. She never did. Cassie called Penelope every day for a week but always got the answering machine. She sent a letter of apology. After a couple of weeks, they finally talked, but Penelope wouldn't talk about the night of the broken dinner date. They never again had dinner or talked on a personal level. If they saw each other at a social event or at the home of a mutual friend, they were polite and distant. Though Cassie had tried, she couldn't get through the wall that Penelope had put up.

What happened to this friendship? It could have been the result of walls on the level of Internal/External Boundaries in the category of Threshold. Penelope had a certain value of shared effort in friendship: in this case, who traveled to see the other. Either she didn't clearly communicate this to Cassie or Cassie ignored it; the experiential definition of this value was rather rigid and did not allow for flexibility. When Cassie didn't show that night, Penelope went through the threshold concerning this friendship. She put up walls and that was the end of it. Cassie also bore responsibility, because she ignored the consequences of her never going out to visit Penelope in the suburbs. She had put up a wall between her behavior and the impact on Penelope's feelings. This is an example of Causality where the walls distort and virtually eliminate the normal cause and effect experience.

This friendship may not have been deep enough to survive this critical misunderstanding, or perhaps a meaningful and long-lasting friendship was lost because of a lack of awareness and understanding resulting from the presence of walls. The walls were not between the two women but around a value (Penelope's) and between a behavior (Cassie's) and its consequences.

Business and professional relationships can be complex and challenging even though they are constrained to one particular area of life. Therefore, Contextual Boundaries are extremely important in your work life. No matter how "close" you get to your boss, employee, or colleague, you must always remember the context you're in. Even if the person becomes part of your personal life, at work that context has to take precedence over the personal relationship. That's one of the reasons why "office affairs" are not usually a good idea. The personal emotions often overwhelm the work context, and things can get very messy. When the boundaries between work life and personal life are blurred, the results can be resentment among other employees, lack of discipline, and impaired performance.

When you travel with colleagues or your boss, the normal constraints of the office often disappear. You may become too familiar or personal. You may forget what the purpose of the trip is, why you are on it, and the rules of appropriate behavior and expectations in a work context.

A boss has multiple responsibilities: to keep people on track, motivated, and organized; to produce for the company; and to maintain positive feelings among the staff. The boss must evaluate, critique, praise, encourage, and discipline. In order to do this successfully, if you are the boss, you need to have boundaries. When you become too detached or have too solid a wall, you begin to treat people like objects. They respond with resentment and frustration.

It's impossible to keep morale and enthusiasm high under these circumstances.

> I know an extremely successful account executive in the advertising industry who recently told me that he had begun to doubt himself, even though he knew he was excellent at his job and that his clients loved him. He had worked for this company for four years, had brought in many new and high-profile clients, and had made a lot of money for the company and himself, but his bosses had never once said to him "good job." He said that they had never expressed any appreciation for his work, and he realized that he wanted some recognition. It was as important as the money he made, because without it he felt used—like an object. This situation was so deeply affecting his self-confidence that he left that company and found another job. His bosses lost a valuable asset because they had isolated themselves behind walls, built perhaps of arrogance, unawareness, or historic patterns of behavior.

Do you ever overreact when your boss or colleague points out something you forgot to do or a mistake you made? Is the person truly being rude or abusive or totally disappointed in you? Or have you lost your boundaries? Perhaps your boss reminds you of your mother with her frown and pressed lips, or your father who you could never seem to please. You could be losing the distinction between your *own* internal self-judgment and the external comments of the other as you mind read what they "really" mean. These are examples of loss of boundaries through Projection/Isolation or Mode.

> My friend Claudia was describing how she really didn't like her secretary, Liz. Claudia felt that Liz was disrespectful and could not or would not take her feedback. Liz continued to do things her way, no matter how many times Claudia explained how she wanted them done, and then pouted or complained about Claudia to her co-workers. I asked Claudia why she just didn't fire Liz, and Claudia said that she felt that it was her fault—that somehow she wasn't doing something right. As we talked about this, I learned that Claudia's parents had blamed her whenever there were problems between them. She grew up with the distorted idea that when something went wrong in a relationship, it was her fault. She had swallowed whole the false causality they had projected onto her.

She now assumed that the breakdown of her relationship with Liz was her fault. This is a case of boundary loss in the category of Causality. It really was much simpler than that: Liz was insubordinate and clearly needed to find another job. Sometimes a cigar is just a cigar!

Transference and countertransference are not limited to the therapeutic context; they occur frequently in the workplace. Countertransference occurs when you lose your boundaries because a person or a situation reminds you of something in your past, and you react to that rather than the present person or situation. This is the Internal/External loss of boundaries in the category of Time—between past and present. When someone treats you as though you are someone else in his life, it is transference for that person; he is actually reacting to that person and not to you. He is transferring his feelings about this other person onto you. This is the loss of Internal/External boundaries in the category of Projection/Isolation. This is made doubly more difficult to handle because usually you're not aware that it's happening. Whenever your responses seems overly intense, ask yourself if your response is appropriate to the circumstances; if not, ask yourself if this person or situation reminds you of anyone else in your life or if there are other times when you react like this. If you're unaware that this is happening, you may flip from projecting to isolation—building walls in order to protect yourself. You may stop responding inappropriately, but you also become less flexible or available. You are more detached from the people around you, which will affect your work and motivation.

Whenever people are working for you or reporting to you, it's useful to pay attention to how they relate to time. If they tend to lose boundaries between the *past* and the *present*, they'll continue to feel bad about a mistake they've made for a long time, and they will have trouble maintaining their self-confidence and getting on with the next project. When you notice this, be sure to use the past tense in your communication and encourage them to do the same when referring to that mistake. Keep reminding them, "That was in the past, today is now and different." If they get discouraged by present obstacles, remind them of other problems in the past that they've overcome. This will help them to use their past as a resource rather than put walls between the past and the present.

Painting a vivid picture of the goal you've set for your employees helps them stay motivated, on track, and connected to the future. Keep reminding them that what they do today is moving them closer to the realization of that goal; this further reinforces the connection between the present and future. Burn-out often occurs when there is no distinction made between what you're doing now and the effects in the future. People get totally absorbed by the pressures and necessities of the present and work nonstop until they drop. They wall off any future consequences to their health, family life, and total well-being, or they wall off their work context from all other contexts. Burn-out reduces efficiency and productivity, increases turnover and the loss of talented workers, and creates a tense and frantic environment. You can help your colleagues and employees to remember that today is not forever and that the future is not today; they have time to accomplish and breathe. To be achievable, a goal must be communicated in a specific and vivid way and put into the future—with some space between now and then. Otherwise people won't connect with the future and won't become motivated, or the goal may be experienced as too close—right on top of them, suffocating them—which creates frantic rather than efficient behavior.

What does "living your life" mean? Every person probably has a somewhat different answer, but doesn't it in some way mean harmony—a flow between work, family, and social environments, between mental, physical, emotional, and spiritual, between peace and passion? Consider the boss who is a workaholic because he has lost the distinction between who he is and his job. "I am my job—I am my company." "I am a vice president." "I am a lawyer, a doctor, an engineer."

> Gil was a smart, ambitious rising star in the chiropractic school where he was the business administrator. He had no other life but that school—he worked 60 hours or more a week, never took vacations, and expected everyone around him to do the same. Gil had accomplished a great deal for the school: he doubled student registration, increased the school's visibility in the community, and developed a viable alumni organization and fund-raising drives. In short, he had taken a small, struggling school and put it on the map. At what price? Because Gil's identity was the school, he neglected all other aspects of his life. His wife was about to leave him, he had

hypertension and high blood pressure, and the environment in his office was downright hostile. The people who worked for him were miserable—unless they had been there for less than six weeks. He kept pushing them to do more, never seemed satisfied, and got very cranky if anyone took a personal day or wanted a vacation after a year of nonstop work.

When there are no boundaries between your work and who you *are*, the consequences negatively affect not only your own well-being but that of the people who work for you and with you. Besides having no boundaries between you and your job, you have walls between "you as your job" and other people. They become objects to be moved around and used to further your ambitions; there's no connection to them as human beings with their own lives and interests. It may be exciting to work with someone like this, especially when she or he is successful, but it rarely succeeds over the long term. Success is great, but so are respect, appreciation, true teamwork, and a supportive environment. When you're passionate about your work, extremely ambitious and hard working, remember you are not your work: your work is one of the important ways in which you express yourself in the world. You are much more than your work, and the people around you are individuals who deserve your attention and consideration.

Communication is the essential ingredient and foundation upon which relationships are built. Communication has many verbal and nonverbal forms but we seem to depend mostly on verbal communication (words). When you are communicating, you are sending both *spoken* and *unspoken* messages. It is critical when you're relating to another person that you are aware of the message you want to send under the actual words you are saying. You want to make the distinction between what you say and the message you want to send. Only with awareness of the boundaries between these two can you know whether your message has been received by the other person. If it hasn't, you have the choice to change the words and/or how the words are delivered in order to get your intended message across.

The distinction between the intended (deeper) message and the surface message is important in all types of relationships.

Patricia was a supervisor in a midsized brokerage firm. Paul was her assistant, and both were very busy. Patricia wanted Paul to know that she appreciated his work. After a particularly hectic day, as she was sorting through incoming messages she said to him, "How's that new project with the traders coming along?" She asked this with a fast tempo while looking at her computer screen and jotting down notes to herself. He answered in a monotone, "Fine." The message she wanted to send was, "I'm interested in how you're doing and want you to know I appreciate your hard work." Paul did not get that message. If she had asked him how she could have asked the question and gotten her intended message across, he would have told her to slow down her tempo and to look at him. Patricia hadn't made the distinction between the spoken and unspoken message, as to her they were the same. They weren't to Paul. Without these boundaries, Patricia missed an opportunity to develop a more positive relationship with Paul, and perhaps this miscommunication planted a seed of dissatisfaction that would ultimately cause difficulties.

I am convinced that people who have mutually satisfying and caring relationships have an unconscious awareness of boundaries, of respecting separateness and allowing connection. Without this essential ingredient, connected relationship cannot happen.

Once upon many times baby eaglets learn to fly. When male and female eagles mate, they remain together for their entire lives. They carefully choose where to build their nest, and they spend weeks building their nest. Usually they choose a site on the top or edge of a high, sheer cliff. It must be in a place that is protected from their predators and near a source of food. It has to be large enough to accommodate the eagles and their babies, and it must be sturdy and secure enough to withstand the harsh elements of wind and rain.

When the nest is prepared and ready, the eggs are laid and the incubation period begins. Male and female take turns sitting on the eggs and hunting for food. Eventually, the eggs are ready to hatch; sometimes the eaglet has a hard time breaking the shell, so mother or father has to carefully—very carefully—help to free the baby. Mother and father share equally the responsibility of caring for two or three very hungry eaglets. It is a good thing there are two of them, because eaglets need a tremendous amount of food and they are almost constantly hungry! They've always got their mouths open, and by turns the parents are hunting and returning with food from dawn until dusk.

One day mother eagle looks at father eagle and says, "I think they're ready." This means it's time for the eaglets to learn how to fly. Mother chooses one and carries him in her claws far up into the sky, much higher than their nest. Father flies right next to them and, when they reach a certain height, he signals mother and she releases the baby eaglet. Since the heaviest part of him is his head, he falls like a stone plummeting straight for the earth far below. As the eaglet falls, the air rushing up at him begins to ruffle his feathers until it catches under some of his wing feathers. Gradually the force of the air lifts the underside of one wing, and this starts to slow down his descent ever so slightly. He feels himself tilted to one side and then the other as the air catches his other wing. By now, the air under his wings has slowed him down enough for him to lift his head and look around. As he does, he discovers he can move his wings and propel himself forward instead of just spiraling down. He begins to experiment with different movements and finds that he can turn and even fly upwards! And there are his parents circling slowly just above him. Pretty soon he's turning and swooping and having lots of fun. He's very excited; flying feels so good!

After a few more turns in the blue sky, his parents head back to their nest with the eaglet following. Showing the eaglet how to land inside the nest is quite a feat, but when they're finally all safely back in the nest, he hops to the edge of the nest, looks down and then looks up at the sky where they just came from. He remembers being let go to fall like a stone toward the earth. He says to his parents, "How could you just drop me into space like that? How did you know I'd be all right?" His mother and father look at him solemnly, and his mother answers, "Well, we haven't lost one yet."

Chapter VIII

Boundaries and Parts

The many different aspects of a person's personality are called parts, and these parts create an inner system that can be described by the metaphor of an inner family of parts. This chapter discusses how this "inner family" functions much like an external family and how boundaries, no boundaries, and walls affect the inner world and mental health of a person. Within the framework of this metaphor is an analysis of what parts are, how they function, and how to communicate with them.

"Part of me would like to get another job, but ..." "I don't like the way that part of her ignores tradition." "It's amazing how he can switch gears: one minute he's engaged and present and the next he's detached and totally involved in his own agenda." "I'm really quite content in my new life, but sometimes there's a part of me that wonders what I'm missing."

You often hear people talk about *parts* of themselves or others, how a part is doubting or driving them or is conflicted about a decision they've recently made. What does this mean? What is this notion of a part when referring to aspects or differences in the same personality? One of the definitions of the verb "to part" is "to separate." I'm using part more as a noun: a part of a person that has behaviors and emotions and thought patterns that are different from the rest of the person. However, the part also serves the function of separating certain emotions, behaviors, thoughts, and attitudes from others. Granted, each individual is one whole person, although you may often feel and think and behave very differently under different circumstances and in different situations. It would be a rare person who could claim that he feels, thinks, and acts in the same way *all* the time! Sometimes you are serious and practical, other times you are silly and frivolous, then kind and patient though sometimes mean and selfish. Sometimes you are content and at peace with yourself and the world, other times you're frustrated, bored, and irritable; your moods change as do your thoughts and responses. You may be one whole person, but there are many aspects to you which I call parts.

This concept has been around for a long time. Sigmund Freud, the father of psychoanalysis, referred to parts of people as their "actors." Carl Jung, a disciple of Freud until going his own way and creating the Jungian approach to psychoanalysis, used the word "parts" when describing the many different aspects of personality and archetypes. Transactional Analysis, an approach to psychotherapy created by Eric Berne, MD, divides people into five parts: the critical and nurturing parent, the adult, the adapted and the natural child. Gestalt, a psychotherapy approach developed by Fritz Perls, speaks of two parts: top dog and underdog. Over the last 150 years, psychology practitioners have often referred to aspects of personality or "parts." Carl Jung said, "Parts of the human psyche detach themselves from consciousness and lead an autonomous life of their own" (*Psychological Factors Determining Human Behaviour*). He was not describing multiple personality as a pathology but rather how regular, healthy people can have many different aspects to their personality.

Taking this idea of parts a step further, I have created a metaphor of the "inner family of parts." Everyone has one, and your mental health depends upon how functional your inner family is. You have many parts: the older you get and the more experiences you have, the richer the tapestry of your life becomes and the more parts you develop. These parts create an inner system that functions much like a real, external family. When the system is functioning, the family is connected and communicating; when it is dysfunctional, the family is disconnected and broken. (Broken is not meant to describe a divorced or one-parent family, and it has nothing to do with the adults' sexual orientation or legal status.)

Parts come into being in several ways:

1. Parts are the result of the official roles you play in society: wife, father, mother, lover, sister, brother, daughter, son, doctor, lawyer, manager, secretary, truck driver, farmer, chef, teacher, boss, sculptor, playwright, and so forth. There are also unofficial roles that you play in your family, social circle, or

workplace such as nurturer, peacemaker, joker, bad boy/girl, troublemaker, mediator, fighter, doer, player, and all the other unlabeled roles you assume because you're good at them or they keep you safe or loved. These roles become such an important part of your life that an inner part is created to run this external role.

2.   Parts are created from certain recurring emotions that are not appropriate to the present situation; they are not a natural response to a particular situation. They are responses to past situations or future possibilities that are actually symptoms of your hidden fears or desires. For example, it's natural to feel fear if you hear footsteps in an empty house at night when you're not expecting anyone or to feel depressed when the grant you worked on for two years is turned down. It is not a natural response to feel depressed because your colleague at work got a smile from your boss and you did not, or to get into a state of panic when in a new learning situation. Confusion in that context is a natural response; panic is not! There are no bad emotions; uncomfortable ones, yes, but not bad ones. Bad implies wrongness, that you shouldn't have them. For any emotion you can name, there are circumstances in which it is a normal, natural human reaction. It is essential to your mental health to be aware of and to make distinctions or boundaries between appropriate emotions (a natural response to the given situation) and inappropriate emotions (responses that do not match the external circumstances). These recurring inappropriate emotions are valuable symptoms of your emotional health, just as physical symptoms communicate important information about your physical health. They contain information essential for your evolution as a human being. And for each of these recurring emotions, there is a corresponding inner part that is responsible for that emotion. (I will go into more depth about appropriate and inappropriate emotions in Chapter 10.)

3.   Parts are born in reaction to a specific experience. An ongoing painful situation with an alcoholic parent may result in the development of a part that must always be alert and prepared for the very worst. This preparedness is useful in anticipating difficulties and developing options to deal with them. However, too much emphasis on being prepared can suffocate

spontaneity and risk taking. A child or young person who is ignored by the adults in her life may develop a part that detaches from emotions and lives only in her head.

> When Connie was 4 years old, she was shopping with her mother in a large store. Somehow they got separated and Connie became lost and very frightened. She noticed some other children with adults and followed them until she got up enough courage to talk to them. She asked them to help her find her Mommy, and eventually they did. To this day, when Connie is frightened, this part will get her to talk to others and ask for help. This part is responsible for the courage to reach out to others and has been a valuable resource for Connie. All your parts are potentially valuable, even the ones that seem destructive and negative.

In order to truly know yourself and your inner world, it is essential that you become aware of your parts: the obvious ones that jump out at you as soon as you consider the possibility of parts, the hidden ones you're afraid of, the ones you'd like to get rid of, and, as you explore this inner family, the ones that you had never been aware of before. Try this exercise. Sit quietly for ten minutes, and imagine you're in a large house that is somehow familiar but one you've never really explored before. You know that each room, each closet, and each area represents a part of you. Allow yourself to begin to wander through this house, reacquainting yourself with the rooms (parts) you know very well. You can open doors you've never opened before and experience rooms or closets that are dark and scary, or loud, big, and overpowering, or ones that flit by quickly like wisps of clouds or ghosts. Then in a special, blank book make a list of your parts—the ones you can name so far—and describe your relationship with each. Do you like the part? Does the part trust you? Is it a disgusting part? Is it a funny one? When does it come out? When does it appear and express itself? With others? Alone? Do you want to kill it? Do you want to nourish it? Remember, there are no bad parts. Create and develop this book of your parts.

⌒⟶

A part is made of two elements: its purpose and its manifestation. The purpose is the end to be attained, or the reason for which it was created, which usually falls into one of two categories: motivation or protection. The second element, the manifestation, is how the part expresses itself, the internal thoughts, emotions, or external behavior designed to accomplish the part's purpose. Every part has a purpose or an intention that is positive within the larger framework of the inner family of parts. The manifestation of that purpose is sometimes negative or even self-destructive. Perhaps you have a part that is your "judge" or critic. The way this part expresses itself may be in a voice that says "You can't do that," "You don't know enough," "You're not smart, clever, creative enough," which is negative. What is its purpose? To motivate you to reach your potential, and that's positive.

The part's negative message challenges you and keeps you striving to do better and better which fulfills its positive purpose. But at what price? The judge is not a bad part; it is trying to do something positive for you but uses a negative behavior to accomplish this. I know many people who have several advanced degrees, or have written many books or reached important goals, who still feel as though their achievement is not enough—that they're not *enough*. Often they have a judge part that, no matter what they have done, continues to express itself by saying, "You're not (something) enough" or "You can't do that!" To enjoy their achievements and find satisfaction within themselves, they must make friends with their judge part. They must honor its positive intention and negotiate respectfully to alter its behavior.

I can't emphasize enough the importance of separating *how* a part manifests itself from its positive purpose. This purpose may not necessarily be positive for others, but it is always intended to take care of the person in some positive way. Depression could positively serve the person by getting him to change something in his life. The positive purpose of avoiding commitment could be to protect the person from being rejected. A very fast tempo can protect someone against feeling emotional pain. Working excessively protects against the anxiety of the emptiness of life. Seeing yourself as ignorant motivates you to study harder.

> Shamus loved his job. He sold high-tech software and enjoyed the challenges of working with different personalities, moving around to different offices, and the edginess of constant competition. He

was good at what he did, and he knew it! His biggest problem was occasional migraine headaches. Whenever one started, he'd have to go to bed for 48 hours. Shamus was compulsive about his work—he was nearly always working. One day, while driving from one customer site to another, he felt the telltale signs of a migraine coming on: pressure across the top of his head, slightly blurred vision, and nausea. He had recently learned something about this parts work and decided that he had nothing to lose by trying it. Feeling kind of foolish, he started to talk to the part responsible for the headache. "I know you have some positive purpose, so let me know what it is and maybe we can work something out." He suddenly realized that the headaches slowed him down so that he got some rest—he was forced to! And, he got to be home with his family. He promised the part that he would take the next day off and rest if the part would stop the headache and let him visit his next customer. He promised he would go right home after that. Magically, the headache disappeared, he saw his customer, and made a big sale. He promptly forgot his promise and said to himself, "Jack's office is only ten miles from here—I haven't seen him in awhile—maybe I'll just drop by and tell him about that new gizmo." Bam! The headache was back! He said, "Okay part, okay! I hear you loud and clear—I'm going home now, and I will take tomorrow off!" Shamus was finally learning to respect this part of himself.

Separating the *purpose*—which is always positive—from the *way* the *part* expresses itself makes it easier to accept the concept that there are no bad parts. When you discover and truly accept the positive purpose of a part, you begin to relate to it with appreciation, and only then can you change the behavior. Any new behavior must honor and accomplish the part's original purpose, or the change will not take root or last. To make friends with your parts, establish communication, and build relationships based on mutual respect, you must begin by separating purpose from behavior—creating boundaries. This is the foundation of self-esteem.

Remember that each of your parts is a member of your inner family of parts. Like any real-life family, it is a system, and what happens to or with one member affects the entire family.

Years ago I had the good fortune of attending several seminars given by Salvadore Minuchin, MD, who has been a research and clinical professor at leading American universities and is an outstanding clinician. He is the author of many books, including the seminal work, *Family Therapy*. A concept that intrigued me about his work was his emphasis on what makes a family system functional rather than how to fix the dysfunctional or broken family. I have adapted from his work three principles for the functional inner family of parts. These principles can apply equally to the inner family as well as to the external family.

Principles Underlying a Functioning Family

1. *Each member's existence must be acknowledged and appreciated as unique and deserving.* From the tiniest infant to the most ancient great-grandmother, each member must be recognized as having the right to exist and given the space to develop and live as a separate individual. This means being separate from and connected to all other members of the family, or in the case of the internal system of parts (the inner family), to the other parts and to the whole person. In Chapter 7, I discussed the impact of boundaries on family relationships. Now I want to emphasize how boundaries impact each person's internal family of parts. How your parts are accepted and appreciated (boundaries), isolated and denied (walls), or mashed together and not differentiated (loss of boundaries) affects your overall mental health, your self-esteem, and your success or failure in the world.

When you attempt to get rid of a part—sometimes this is disguised as stopping a destructive behavior, you are doomed to failure. A part is created to take care of you in some way and to fulfill its positive purpose. If you try to interfere with this, the unconscious mind's survival mechanisms are triggered. If you don't discover and honor the positive purpose, it is as though you are trying to kill off a part of yourself. The internal family system successfully resists this attempt to get rid of a part of it, and the part actually gets stronger and more resistant. Because the part has a purpose, the greater the pressure to get rid of it, the more it pushes back. You may have found that the more you try to get rid of a behavior, the more persistent it becomes. When you are successful at changing a behavior, what you have actually done—consciously or unconsciously—is honor the positive purpose and substituted an alternative, more positive behavior that accomplishes the original purpose.

Fear, hatred, disgust, or shame with a part result in walls being built around that part so that the part cannot connect with the inner system of parts or the whole person. Every part is a potential resource and when a part is walled off, the whole person is deprived of its resources. The flow of energy within that person's unconscious and between his conscious and unconscious minds is disrupted. It is like a family trying to act as though a member doesn't exist or is dead. The fabric of the family's existence is torn.

Walls are sometimes created by excessive separation between one context and another. A part that represents certain abilities or skills in one particular situation will remain disconnected and unavailable in other situations. For example, a young man might have unlimited patience and understanding when working with disadvantaged children. However, when coping with personal issues such as paperwork, filling out forms, or household chores, he blows up at the slightest obstacle. His patience—or, if you will, the part representing his patience—is accessible only in one context and not available in others because of walls.

People deal with trauma by detaching from the part of them going through the trauma. That part then becomes walled off from the rest of the person, and this detachment eventually becomes permanent. This walling-off is helpful during the trauma itself, but over time, it becomes a negative drain on the system. No matter what the reason for isolating and walling-off a part, the effect is not healthy. It can result in the loss of self-confidence, undesirable physical symptoms, inappropriate emotional responses, loss of self-control, unexplained depression or anxiety, eating disorders, learning difficulties, lack of motivation, and sexual dysfunction.

A lack of boundaries between parts means there are little or no distinctions between them, and one or more of the weaker or less-confident parts can get swallowed up by the bigger, louder parts. When you mush elements together, you get a crumbly mess; when you mush parts together, you get a confused mess. One part can overshadow the other, and the so-called weaker part's abilities are lost to the whole person—even the stronger part is weakened and confused by the lack of separation. If the mushing of parts is more or less equal, this still results in lack of clarity and definition of resources and purpose. Parts can get hidden in the crumbly mess just as much as they can behind walls.

Within your inner family of parts, there are walls, no boundaries, or boundaries, and they can change your inner visual and auditory experience in the following ways. With walls, your internal images tend to be a combination of one or more of these elements: shades of black, gray, and white; seeing self in the image as small or distant; seeing two-dimensional, framed images; abstract representations of self and others such as stick figures or cartoon images. You might have the impression that there is a transparent, acrylic glass wall between the part or memory and you. There might be a blank screen. Auditorily, you might hear constant chatter, talking to yourself and commenting on what you and others in the memory or the present experience are doing, saying, and feeling. Compared to your normal self-talk, this chatter is usually faster in tempo and louder in volume.

When boundaries are lost among parts or between the whole self and a part, you have an internal experience of tunnel vision or hearing—a distortion of the relationship of foreground to background. When you're reliving a memory, it's as though you're really there in the memory, seeing through your eyes, hearing through your ears (you do not see or hear yourself), and a foreground figure becomes abnormally larger, brighter, clearer or louder than the background figures.

Your internal representation of boundaries is similar to your external experience of boundaries; you have peripheral seeing and hearing, which results in a panoramic internal visual and auditory experience. Images are in normal, life-like colors and three-dimensional, and there is a natural relationship of foreground to background. You can easily move from seeing yourself in the internal experience to stepping into the experience where you see, hear, and feel what's around you.

To know yourself, it is necessary to get to know your inner family of parts, including the parts that are hidden behind walls and those parts mashed together and obscured in the crumbly mess. As you discover, accept, and appreciate all your parts, they will begin to trust you and become more accessible to you.

2. *There must be an appropriate hierarchy of roles within the family system.* Although every part is worthy, parts are not equal. Each part deserves respect and appreciation, but the importance, responsibility, and expression of each part will depend upon the circumstances and context. For example, in the external family, the infant rightfully takes up a lot of time and space. He or she occupies a place of extreme importance but has no responsibility to pay the bills or put food on the table. The young adolescent can be expected to contribute some time and effort to household chores but should not be responsible for the family's general welfare. A parent is responsible for the welfare of the children, the financial stability of the family, and its emotional well-being, but she should not depend on her children for her emotional nourishment. In other words, parents must take on the role of parents and not abdicate their responsibilities to their children. The grandfather is an important and respected figure within the family, although unless absolutely necessary because of special circumstances he does not take the central role of daily caregiver. Each member of a family must have a recognized role that is appropriate to his or her age, physical, mental, and emotional abilities, the circumstances of the immediate situation, and the needs of the system.

> Cleo's husband died when her son Aiden was 10 months old and her daughter Annabelle 11 years old. There was no inheritance, pension, or insurance, and so she had to work in order to support her family. For the first couple of years, things were very difficult emotionally and financially; there was no money for baby-sitters, so Annabelle had to take care of Aiden while Cleo was at school or work. Cleo sometimes leaned on Annabelle for emotional support. This was appropriate only because of the drastic circumstances and only as a limited and temporary measure. As soon as the financial situation improved, most of the baby-sitting responsibilities were lifted from Annabelle's shoulders and, with time, her mother got stronger and no longer needed emotional support from her daughter. If the situation had continued for too long, with Annabelle

taking on too much of a parental role, this family would have become dysfunctional.

Each part within the inner family must have an appropriate role and must know when to express herself and when to remain in the background. When I'm teaching, it's appropriate that my teacher part predominates (with a little help from my creative and actor parts). It would not be appropriate for my lazy part to come out when I'm teaching—the part that likes to space out, daydream, and read mystery novels!

> Mr. Greene was the administrator of a large and rapidly growing company. He was visionary, hard working, and well organized. The only problem was that he would sometimes become bored and let day-to-day details slip through the cracks. Sometimes he was involved and consistent, but at other times, he was inattentive and would come to work late or not at all. He was sabotaging his career and the company; morale was bad and profits were down. Mr. Greene had a part named Sonny whose purpose was to keep him happy and fulfilled. Sonny liked to fly planes and write poetry and go for long hikes by himself. When he didn't get to do this, he became very bored and distracted. Mr. Greene had forgotten about his Sonny part in his rush to climb the corporate ladder, and Sonny had to get his attention one way or another! Because Sonny was expressing himself at inappropriate times, it was necessary to negotiate between Sonny and Mr. Greene's ambitious part. They had to agree to give Sonny time to relax and have fun so that he didn't show up when his behavior would be destructive and thereby create chaos.

You can't have "the joker" show up at a funeral, the "flirt" attend a meeting of the bank's board of directors, or the "scared little girl" appear when comforting your 3 year old. There must be a hierarchy of parts that is congruent with the circumstances. The part you are expressing, the part that is driving you at any moment in time, must match the situation. The part must have boundaries, and it must be recognized, accepted, and connected to the whole system.

You might ask yourself, "How do I learn what is appropriate?" "Who's more important: me or others?" "When do I follow my needs and wants, and when do I put others' before mine?" "Do I need a manager part, an appropriateness commissioner, a values coordinator?"

You learn which parts are appropriate in which situations through experience. Initially, your conscious mind is aware of the consequences of certain parts expressing themselves. With time, these learnings become unconscious, and a part is created that could be called a "manager," a "coach," a "values maven," or whatever name you want to give him or her. Questions like "When do I put your wants before others?" are more complicated than "When do I express my joker part?" Conflicts can arise between your manager and other parts, but as long as there are boundaries between them, the conflicts can be worked out. Unresolved conflicts arise when a part has walls or no boundaries. The manager part is not the boss; it is more like the conductor of an orchestra. She does not actually create or make the music; she directs the various parts when to play, how loud, how fast, and when to stop and quietly wait for the next cue to appear. Without the orchestra, the conductor has nothing to do. Without the conductor, the orchestra can still make music—perhaps not as smoothly or coherently, but it still exists and can express itself, however imperfectly.

Knowing when to express and give priority to what part depends on your values and your personal experiential definition of these values. The standards used to measure your behavior or another's, to determine whether something is desirable or not, dangerous or safe, appropriate or not, evolves over time. Difficulties and confusion arise when you have either walls or no boundaries around these values. The former causes you to stubbornly hold on to your idea of what your value means in spite of experience and evidence to the contrary. With the latter, you're easily swayed by another's opinion or the emotions of the situation. Both these boundary distortions will interfere with learning the appropriate hierarchy of your different parts in different situations. When your values have boundaries, you can be both flexible and stable.

3. *There must be a structure to support communication between and among members of the family.* Most of us would agree that sharing a common language and possessing the ability to speak and to hear does not guarantee communication. This is true both in

an external family and within an inner family of parts. What is human communication? What does it mean to communicate? I'm not using the word "communicate" to describe technological transfer of information. I'm referring to the messages between two or more human beings: one person sending a message and the other or others receiving that message and responding, creating a continuous loop. Communication is like playing catch: you throw the ball and the other catches it. If you keep throwing the ball 30 feet away from where the catcher is, it's not going to be any fun. Pretty soon you won't be playing catch anymore, you'll be fighting! Or if you stand two feet apart and gently lob the ball into the catcher's hands, you'll both get very bored and stop playing.

The following applies equally to communicating with other people and communicating with your internal parts. To communicate, you must acknowledge that you are separate from the one with whom you want to communicate, that he is worthy of your effort, and that you really want to communicate with him. In other words, you must have boundaries. You must pay attention to his responses. Since it's only by his responses that you will know whether or not he's gotten your message, you must really listen to him rather than being busy inside your head, defending yourself or constructing your next answer. You cannot really listen to the other and be talking to yourself about what he's saying or what you're going to say—this will create walls. If you assume that you know what he's going to say before he says it, or what he really means before he has a chance to explain, you've lost boundaries, and you're certainly not communicating with him.

Bridges of communication have to be built between your conscious mind and your parts, and among your parts. As surprising as it may seem, your parts do not necessarily know a lot about each other or how to communicate with each other. The secret to communicating with your parts is boundaries. Boundaries provide each part the space to be and the permeability to receive and send messages.

The foundation of communicating is the absence of judgment. When you put judging aside and can let go of the need to be right, you can be truly present and open to possibilities. You can accept the other's right to her opinions—you can really listen and hear her. Acceptance does not mean agreement, it simply means receiving the other. At any given moment, you can choose to make a judgment, but as soon as you do, you put a stop sign in front of any real communication. This is especially true when communicating with your parts. Communication is a two-way street, a give and take.

Putting aside judgment means nonpolar thinking. To engage in polar thinking is either/or, yes/no, good/bad, right/wrong, digital/analog. It is the two opposing ends of a continuum. Nonpolar or optional thinking is what's in-between these two opposites. Polar thinking results from walls and optional thinking from boundaries. Both polar and nonpolar thinking are legitimate choices, and both are useful and beneficial at different times. I am not saying that nonpolar is better than polar or that you should *always* engage in nonpolar thinking! I have found, however, that when communicating with your parts, polar thinking is rarely useful. The point is to be aware of how you're thinking and decide how you want to think, given whatever situation you're in. Whenever you're having trouble communicating, when you think your message is not getting across, notice whether you're in a polar or nonpolar thinking frame. If it's polar, ask yourself if it's really important to be right (and the other person wrong). If it is, continue to do what you're doing, but understand that you're judging, not communicating. If being right is not that important, step back and listen to yourself for a moment. Eliminate words such as good/bad, right/wrong, or yes/no. Tell yourself that the other person, or the part, has a right to a different opinion and listen to her.

To practice making the distinction between polar and nonpolar thinking, imagine a situation in which your neighbor is putting his garbage out so close to the entrance to your driveway that it's practically on your property. Every time it is picked up, some of his garbage is invariably spilled onto your driveway. Doing polar thinking, you would say to yourself or anyone around to listen, "This is not right, I should not have to pick up his garbage!" After this happens six or seven times, you're getting really angry, and when you next see your neighbor, you're ready to yell at him. After all, what's right is right! It's your property, and it's absolutely wrong of him to disrespect you and your rights in this way. If polar thinking was suddenly unavailable to you, how and what would you think? Try this along with me: "Perhaps he doesn't realize where exactly the property line is. Perhaps he doesn't realize the garbage is spilling onto my driveway or understand fully how troubling it is to me. Maybe together we can build an attractive enclosure for both of our garbage cans, or talk to the garbage collectors, or find another place to put the garbage, or change garbage companies." I'm sure there are many other options. The point is to think in this way rather than jumping immediately to right/wrong judgments.

Polar thinking puts up walls that block other possibilities. Falling into its trap is like falling into a ditch with walls so high that you can see only what's right in front of you. You always have the choice, after checking out other possibilities, to draw that line in the sand and do the right/wrong thing. That's sometimes the best choice, but you'll never know that if you immediately block out all other information with knee-jerk polar thinking.

Give yourself this challenge. In a situation where you go automatically to right/wrong or good/bad thinking, step back for a moment, pretend you cannot think this way and imagine what you would do if you had no access to polar thinking. If you couldn't think, "This is wrong, and I'm right!" or use words such as good/bad or yes/no, how and what do you think?

If you want to get to know your parts, communicate with them, influence them, and benefit from them, you must come from the frame of nonpolar thinking. Creating a structure for communicating with your parts requires a fundamental respect and appreciation for each part. This is not that difficult when you remember that the part always has some positive purpose for you, even if its manifestation appears negative.

The ability to change is equated with growth and evolution. It's been said that change is the only constant in this world; it's perfectly understandable to want to influence and guide others toward positive change. Perhaps you have this desire to make a difference in the world, to help change the world for the better. This is a worthy and honorable cause. When we are engaged in changework, we are acting as change agents; we're helping, guiding, teaching, and influencing others to act, think, and feel in a way that bring positive results.

There is another position you can take beside change agent when communicating with others: Fair Witness. I'm talking about meaningful personal communication rather than simply getting directions, buying a loaf of bread, or getting your telephone repaired. These can be very important, at the moment, but these are exchanges of information that are more impersonal than deeply personal.

The Fair Witness position is one of total lack of self-interest.

When acting as a change agent, it is important to me that I help you, motivate you to act differently or understand something differently. I want to comfort you, to heal you, to impart knowledge that will assist you in achieving your goals. I am involved personally in you changing yourself; there is self-interest in the outcome of our communication, even when my primary goal is your benefit.

In Fair Witness, I am not involved in the outcome; I have no attachment to you changing. This is a position of "not caring"—it does not mean not caring about the humanity of the other but not being attached to helping, fixing, comforting, pleasing, or judging the other. It is a position of total acceptance of the other's anger, pain, desires, confusion, hostility—whatever he is going through, however he is feeling. Fair Witness requires boundaries that allow you to touch and be touched emotionally by the other, not walls that would isolate you, or lack of boundaries that would suck you into the other's feelings and desires. It is not a position of detachment but of involvement and energy—not in the other feeling better or learning something but involvement in the process of the interaction itself and the person. When you are in Fair Witness, you are present, vulnerable to the other, giving and receiving energy. Totally accepting the other without judgment *and* without the need to help, fix, comfort, or please.

You are not just an observer in the Fair Witness position. You are an active participant in the interaction, putting aside any need or desire for the other to learn, change, or feel better. From this position, you can really send the message, "You're okay just the way you are. I accept without any judgment your depression, your rage, your fear, and your pain. These are your feelings, they are not good or bad, they simply are. I am here to be present with you, to bear witness to you, to attest to you and your experience without self-interest or prejudice, with compassion and caring for your whole person."

Why is this a useful position to learn? It allows you the option of acting in a role other than change agent, it gives you access to information and emotions that may otherwise be unavailable, and it keeps you honest. When you get good at something, your ego gets involved, and your sense of self and identity begins to get wrapped up in it. When you're good at helping others to make positive changes in their lives, invariably your ego is fed. This is normal, but are you aware of when you cross the line from wanting to needing to heal someone, to comfort her, to help her? When you need to help someone because it makes you feel worthy or because it feeds your identity, you've crossed that line. The Sufis have a saying that applies here: "Our gifts are our greatest traps." Meaning our strengths, what we're good at, can blind us and disguise self-serving motives. It's normal to feel good about doing something well and achieving your goals, but when those goals involve helping people change, you must be careful about what drives you. Is it the other person's benefit or your ego? By letting go of the need to help, heal, or fix, Fair Witness position cleanses and centers you.

It also supports your message to the other that she is okay exactly as she is. If you're always needing to "change" the other, the message you're sending is that her emotions, her anger or pain are not okay. She's not okay. Sometimes wanting to help or comfort is a sign of caring; sometimes it's really a sign of your discomfort with the other's pain. There are times when just being present (witnessing) without any self-interest (fair) is the most comforting and beneficial gift you can give.

Fair Witness creates a safe, nonjudgmental space in which the person or the part can express themselves. When you are listened to without being helped or judged, you are free to be you, to feel and think and express yourself in ways you may never have before. Fair Witness helps to create a liberating environment in which you can discover your own resources and solutions. You can gain new understandings and draw upon untapped learnings. The most effective resolution to a problem is the one a person comes to himself.

This position is useful to adopt in a variety of situations: in any type of mediation where by definition the mediator must not have any self-interest in the outcome; any time you experience resistance from the other; when you're working harder than the other person to find a solution; when it becomes too important to you to help the other; when one or both parties are caught up in being right; and when working with parts.

It is not useful to stay in Fair Witness most of the time, but it is important to be able to shift into this position whenever you realize it would be beneficial for you, the other person, or the situation. The requirements for this position are as follows:

1. Maintain boundaries.
2. Let go of any attachment to outcomes.
3. Have no need to fix, help, comfort, please, or judge the other.
4. Be present, available, and energized.
5. Stay sensitive to your own need or desire to help, recognizing it when it comes up and shifting back into "not caring/not being attached."

Practice the Fair Witness position by deciding ahead of time when you will do it. For example, you might use it during the first five minutes of a specific interaction you know you will be having or whenever you begin to feel like you're trying too hard to help or convince someone to feel better. In the beginning, limit your time in this position to five minutes or less. Review the main principles of Fair Witness. When you notice the impulse to help, comfort, fix, or judge, accept the impulse, take a breath, and go back into Fair Witness. It is not useful to judge *yourself* for having these impulses. Simply use them as reminders to let go of helping or judging.

Communicating with Your Parts

To realize your potential talents and resources, you must get to know your parts and discover how to communicate with them. The first goal is to accept this idea of the inner family of parts as a metaphor! Within this metaphor, communication flows more readily and otherwise hidden or blocked information is more accessible to you.

You can work with your own parts and, if you're trained in psychotherapy and counseling, you can work with other people's parts. Certain principles underlie both types of work with parts:

1. There are no "bad" parts. Every part has two elements: the positive purpose and the manifestation of this purpose in the form of behaviors, thoughts, or emotions. The positive intention or purpose exists in relation to the psychic structure of the whole person.

2. People and their parts have the inner resources to resolve their problems and achieve their goals, no matter how hidden and inaccessible they seem to be.

3. Your unconscious is trustworthy. Frame and express a clear question to your unconscious and trust that first response before the great censor and doubter, the conscious mind, confuses you.

4. The primary goal of communicating with a part is to create a safe space within which the part can express itself freely, without judgment.

5. Maintain your boundaries, and be alert to whether the part with whom you want to communicate has boundaries, walls, or no boundaries. A part with boundaries is easier to talk to and establish a relationship with. When a part has walls, it will take time and patience to communicate with it—you will have to get that part to trust you before it will come out from behind the walls long enough to truly express itself. This is an excellent opportunity to use the Fair Witness position. When boundaries are lacking, there will be a lot of confusion about

who you're actually talking to. It will seem as though you are with one part and then another comes forth and perhaps even another. Instead of one part, there will seem to be a mush—a crumbly mess—with very little meaningful communication. Take the time to sort out the parts: begin with one, name it, and keep going back to that one. In doing this, you are helping the part define itself and distinguish itself from the other parts. It may be afraid of being separate. You have to reassure the part that it can be connected more profoundly when it is separate.

6. When there is any resistance, hostility, or excessive fear, be ready to let go of any desire to change or help, Use both positions: Fair Witness to create a safe space for the part and get to know him, and change agent to guide the part to a new understanding or behavior.

7. Be honest with the part. Parts are like children—they can smell incongruence and self-serving pretense from a mile away. If you're not authentic, they'll never trust you. Better to admit that you don't know something than to pretend, especially with parts or children!

8. Accept a part's objections, anger, fear, or despair without judgment or interpretation. If a part argues or disagrees with you, back off and understand that what's actually happening is that part doesn't feel safe or really acknowledged. Do not personalize the part's response; accept the response as simply more information about that part.

9. Always use a respectful tonality. Reassure parts that you appreciate that they have a positive purpose, and thank them for being willing to speak with you.

10. Ask for a name and how old the part is. Eventually it will answer. Be patient, as this may take time.

In summary:

1. Accept the metaphor of parts, that you have or the other person has parts and that you can communicate with them.

2. Determine whether the part with whom you want to communicate has boundaries, walls, or no boundaries, and relate to it accordingly.

3. Discover the positive purpose. Ask questions such as, "How has this part benefited me in my life?" Or directly ask the part, "What are you trying to do for me?"

4. Make friends with the part. It's difficult to communicate with an enemy. Start by appreciating the part's purpose.

5. Be open to learning about the part—you may be surprised! Do not think that because it is a part of you or because you have an intuition about the part that you know it. You probably don't!

6. Become familiar with and utilize the Fair Witness position.

Structures for Partswork with Self

1. With any persistent inappropriate emotion or thought pattern (that does not match circumstances), assume there is a part responsible, and begin a conversation with it. Possible questions: "What are you trying to do for me?" "Do you want me to do something different?" "What do you want me to do?" "Do you object to something I'm doing now?" "What can I do for you?" Ask one question and wait for a response. Trust the first response you get.

2. Once you've identified a part you want to learn more about and communicate with, imagine that part living somewhere in your body. Find a specific spot. Then pick an image, a word (which can be the part's name), a sound, and a sensation that represents that part. Practice awareness of all these occurring together until whenever you think of this particular part, you automatically have the image, word, and sensation attached to a specific place in your body. Then ask the part to give you some signal as a means of communication. The signal might be an increase or decrease of a sensation, an increase or decrease of the volume or tempo of a word, or the brightness or size of an image. Trust and follow your part.

3.   Imagine the part with whom you want to communicate in your hand. Give the part a shape, color, size, sound, texture, and weight. Have a conversation with it. Ask your questions, and trust the first responses. This is not a cognitive analysis or an intellectual discussion. Communicate with the part simply to establish a relationship and get to know the part. "Tell me about yourself." "What do you like, or not like?" "What other parts of me do you know, like, and not like?" "Who supports you?" "Who scares you or makes you angry?" "Who judges you?" When asking for any change in a part's behavior, you must first discover and honor the part's positive purpose. You could ask, "How else can you achieve your positive purpose?" You could make some suggestions, making sure that the alternatives honor the part's positive purpose. Always reintegrate the part back into your inner self by bringing your hand holding the part to your chest and holding it there for a moment. Breathe.

Limit the work to five minutes. Always thank the part for communicating with you, no matter how fleetingly or reluctantly, and say something about wanting to continue to get to know the part better and learn about it. One of the most important benefits of this work is that you are creating a safe space, an environment, and an opportunity for the part to express itself. You'll be surprised at how much you'll learn about yourself! And hold fast to the principle that there are no bad parts: each and every one has a positive purpose, and each part of you is potentially your ally. If you're having trouble not judging one of your parts, practice being in the Fair Witness position with the part. Acceptance is not agreement or approval; when you judge your parts, they will not communicate with you, and you'll learn nothing about them or about yourself.

Do not attempt to do partswork with other people unless you are well trained in counseling and psychotherapy.

You might get frustrated, annoyed, or discouraged by a part's objections. It can seem as though they're endless. In meaningful personal communication, objections are not obstacles but clues to what the other person or part needs in order to understand or trust you. In general, objections are signals that the part, or the person doesn't feel acknowledged or understood. This means that you are not getting your message across, especially if your message is one of interest, caring, and respect. Listen carefully to the objection and treat it as an opportunity to learn more about the part and to see things from her point of view. Changing to her point of view results in more information about her, and this leads to increased understanding. When you constantly attempt to "handle" the other's objections, you send the message that her objections are simply obstacles to be overcome rather than something important to her that you want to understand and listen to. Objections are important information about the other that deserve your full attention. This would be an excellent time to step into Fair Witness!

Objections often have to do with personal ecology or the relationships of your interconnected systems. You are the sum of your interconnected internal systems and your external systems: your physical, mental, emotional, spiritual systems, and your family, work, social, community, and global systems. Your systems are separate and connected. They should have boundaries. If there are walls or no boundaries between systems, those systems become dysfunctional, reflecting a disruption in the relationship between systems. For example, when your work and intimate life become one, or you wall off your connection to your physical body, your internal systems are thrown off. Any change that you make is like a stone thrown into a pond; there is a ripple effect, and the slightest change in one system affects all the other systems.

When you make a change in your mental system and begin to think positively about your future, it affects your physical system. Your posture changes, and your breathing and circulation flow more smoothly. Your emotional system is affected because you're feeling happier and more confident. Even your spiritual system may be affected in subtle ways. Your family system may be disrupted because they're used to you being discouraged, and now that you're a more positive person, some family members may feel insecure about the change. At work, colleagues could be threatened by your new more assertive behavior—and so it goes.

You may get an objection from one part of you that wants you to be liked because if you're more self-confident, suddenly some people may not like you as much. This objection does not mean you cannot or should not be more confident about your future. It does mean that you have to be prepared for others' responses and for the consequences of the change, both positive and negative. Objections driven by ecological considerations are important information. They are the ripples that help you refine your goals, weigh the consequences, and keep your life ecological.

Cassandra had been feeling lonely and unloved in her marriage. She had an affair with André, which temporarily relieved these feelings. However, she loved her husband and wanted their relationship to work, so she ended the affair. Several months later she told Martin, her husband, about it, and this precipitated a crisis in their marriage. Cassandra had two parts: the Judge and the Vulnerable part. Both were born when she was a child. The Judge was there to protect her from a very critical mother by criticizing Cassandra before her mother could. This helped her to deal with her mother. Vulnerable protected her from feeling unloved and rejected by merging with others who were hurting, feeling their pain and helping them to feel better. This way Cassandra didn't have to feel her own pain or risk asking for what she wanted and being rejected.

The Judge put up walls between Cassandra and others' criticism, while Vulnerable lost boundaries whenever significant people in her life were upset or in pain. Martin was judgmental, so she related to him by criticizing herself before he could and putting up a wall between them to protect herself from his criticism. When he got hurt (as he was when he found out about the affair), she merged with him and tried to fix his pain. This left him no space to feel his feelings and deal with them himself. When he expressed his anger, Cassandra closed off from him entirely—at the same time criticizing herself for being a horrible person and a terrible wife who deserved to lose everything she cared about.

The walls the Judge put up made it impossible to connect with her husband. Vulnerable avoided possible rejection by feeling his pain instead of hearing him and asking for what she wanted.

With work, Cassandra became aware of when she put up walls and when she lost boundaries with her husband. She made friends with these two parts of herself and learned to appreciate them. She's now beginning to develop boundaries so that she can be separate from Martin and listen to him while staying connected to him. She's learning to accept herself as perfectly human, to express her feelings, and to ask for what she wants. Their marriage has a chance now.

Nathaniel is a three-year-old part of Nate who had stayed quiet and hidden for most of Nate's life. Nate experienced anxiety attacks and periodically became hypochondriacal. He would become convinced that he was having a heart attack or had cancer and go to doctors, who would order all sorts of tests. All these doctors and tests confirmed that there was nothing wrong with him, and he would then feel better for a while. These attacks became more frequent in his early thirties, and he came to consult with me. I introduced him to the concept of parts and taught him how to communicate with them—his inner family. Eventually he became aware of Nathaniel, but this part had put walls up to keep himself safe. At first Nathaniel simply observed our work with other parts but wouldn't communicate directly with either Nate or me. Even so, Nate felt his presence. One day, Nathaniel was willing to talk with me. Nate became Nathaniel; Nathaniel began to trust me and allow me to get to know him as boundaries were developing. He was born when Nate was 3 years old and his mother died suddenly. Nathaniel was very scared and built himself a safe room to hide in; it was small and dark with no windows. But he felt safe in there. He created other parts to do things for him: a 4 year old who loved to play and joke around; Horace, who was serious and practical; and Bonnie, who was creative, painting beautiful pictures and playing the piano. But Nathaniel was too scared to come out of his safe room. As Nate got older, Nathaniel was tired and bored in that dark room, but he didn't have the courage to come out. When he talked to me, he had at least opened the door. He told me that he was responsible for Nate's anxiety and hypochondria (he didn't call it that—he said he made Nate think he was sick) because he wanted Nate to pay attention to him and acknowledge him. Whenever Nate got close to someone, Nathaniel would make him scared that there was something wrong with his body. Nathaniel was protecting Nate from ever being betrayed again, which was how Nathaniel experienced the death of Nate's mother. He was beginning to want to come out of the room, but he was afraid that he and Nate wouldn't survive. He had no experiences of survival. While Nate was growing up, having experiences, some difficult and painful, Nathaniel was behind the walls of his safe room. Together, we made a book that showed and talked about the different experiences Nate had gone through, how he had survived some painful times and had learned and become a stronger and better person. We created images of these experiences that Nathaniel would keep in his special book. Whenever he was scared, he could go back and look at these pictures and feel those strong feelings of survival. Nathaniel was reassured, and he began to come out of his room. Nate began to appreciate this part of himself who sometimes got anxious and thought he was sick. Nate was establishing boundaries between Nathaniel and himself, allowing them to connect. Nathaniel felt more accepted and didn't have to make Nate sick to get his attention.

A few weeks afterward, Nathaniel reported being overwhelmed with his new-found social connections. He wanted some alone-time, some peace and quiet and, yes, safety. He remembered his room as a child, before his mother died, which was full of light, with many windows, painted yellow with white trim and a soft, blue rug on the floor. It had shelves of books and toys and a comfortable bed with a fluffy comforter and pillows. He loved this room and felt very safe there. So Nathaniel created this imaginary but very real room for himself where he could go when feeling overwhelmed or scared. It comforted and reassured him without walling him off from Nate. Pretty smart part, yes?

A part is a discrete aspect of personality with a unique positive purpose within the inner psychic family system that is worthy of respect and appreciation; whose manifestation through behavior, thoughts, beliefs, or emotions can contribute or detract from the overall positive functioning of the whole person. To quote Richard Schwartz, an American psychologist and author, "A part is not just a temporary emotional state or habitual thought patterns. Instead it is a discrete and autonomous mental system that has an idiosyncratic range of emotion, style of expression, and set of abilities, intentions, or functions" (*Internal Family Systems Therapy*, 1995).

Once upon a time, there was a great country filled with many material resources, beautiful lands, rivers, and mountains, and hard-working, attractive people. The only problem in this country was that the people made war on each other. They fought because of the flags they had inherited from their ancestors. Each group had their own flag with a legend handed down from one generation to the next. The flags were beautiful even if the wars fought because of them were not.

The flags represented important traditions and history going back hundreds or even thousands of years. People killed each other in the name of these traditions and stories and their flag. At first glance, the battlefields seemed beautiful, with all those wondrous flags waving in the breeze, but when you looked closer, you saw the blood and the wounded and dead. Those who died on these battlefields seemed willing to suffer and to sacrifice their lives for the flag; many died looking up at their flag. People were proud of their warriors, and thus the great traditions and stories of their flags were preserved.

One day, a large sailing ship appeared on the horizon. As it approached the land, it got bigger and bigger until it came right up to the beach. People came from all parts of the country to gaze at the largest ship anyone had ever seen. A giant man walked down the gangplank. This giant was *very* tall and *very* nice and *very* gentle, He never ate children and was very careful not to step on any of the inhabitants. People got used to him and accepted him while he explored the country and observed the many wars being fought among the people.

As the giant watched, he became quite disturbed by the continuous warring, for, apart from their fighting, the people were good people. He finally made a decision; he began to prepare a great feast and invited everyone in the country. With one of his fingers, he took wild boars and roe-deer to roast on the many fires. With another finger, he made excellent cereals and baked loaves of delicious bread. From his

149

ship, he brought jams, jellies, honey, dried fruits, nuts and pickled vegetables, and finally a huge barrel of good wine.

Everyone came to the feast, enticed by the delicious smells of the cooking and the promise of excellent food and wine. In the middle of this great party while people were eating and drinking with gusto, the giant began to cry.

"What's the matter?" the people asked him. "Everyone is having such a good time. Why are you upset?"

"I don't have a flag for myself," answered the giant.

People felt bad for him because he had given them such a wonderful feast with great food and wine. They wanted him to be happy, so one of the women asked him what he would like. The giant said, "I would love my own huge flag made with all your smaller flags—that would be my dream come true."

Immediately all the women understood what he was doing, and so they gathered all the country's flags and sewed them together. Perhaps because the men had drunk so much of the delicious wine, and maybe because they were a little afraid of the giant, they did not object. The women finished the immense flag that had so many beautiful colors you could not believe it!

The giant was very happy and thanked everyone for the gift with much emotion and sincerity. He took his magnificent flag back to his ship and sailed away over the horizon. Everyone had to say farewell to their *fighting* ancestors, and from that time on there was no more war in that country.

Traditions have changed now, and the women proudly tell their daughters, and their daughters tell *their* daughters the great legend of the flag. And so a better story, and better tradition, has been created.

Adapted from a story by Patrick Condamin

Chapter IX

Boundaries and Identity

The belief about "who I am" or "what the world is" is a self- or world-concept that can be changed since it is only an idea conceived in the mind—and you can change your mind! Walls hold these concepts unchanging and rigidly in place; boundaries allow them to change as they respond to your experiences. This chapter explores what identity is and how you can make it concrete, experiencing it as solid and flexible, encompassing the many dimensions of you.

That deceptively simple question, "Who are you?" is not simple at all. "I'm his mother, her husband, I'm Ted, I'm Betty, I'm Jane, I'm the driver, I'm the owner, I'm Jack's wife, I'm the teacher, I'm the writer." All are legitimate answers to that question, or are they? Are you mother, husband, Jane, the teacher? Yes, you may be, but is that your identity? Have you ever sat down and asked yourself, "Who am I?" You know what you are: a physical body with blond hair and brown eyes, five feet ten inches with short fingers and broad feet—a man who has several roles in life like father, brother, teacher and friend. But who are you?

The question of identity is complex and seemingly endless. The definition of identity is essential beingness. Your essence. That sounds reasonable, but what does it mean? Does it get you any closer to connecting to your identity, experiencing it as something you can hold on to instead of another intellectual concept? I know and you know that you're not just an intellectual concept. To experience your essence, you must give it some definition and shape. You need to differentiate it from the mass of ideas, thoughts, emotions, sensations, beliefs, self-concepts, roles, jobs, and behaviors that make up you. In other words, separate your essence, at least metaphorically, from the background busyness of you.

To do this, let us first examine beliefs. Like everyone else, you have beliefs about your identity. They are likely to be hidden deep in your unconscious mind, but they nonetheless drive your thoughts, emotions, and behavior. Although these beliefs profoundly influence your life, they are not your identity. The dictionary definition of "belief" is a state or habit of mind in which trust or confidence is placed in some person or thing. The dynamic definition that describes the role that a belief has in a person's life is: a generalization you make about yourself and/or the world that takes the form of a rule that guides you to achieve or avoid an important value. For example, the belief, "I'm not lovable," is associated with the value of love, the flip side of which is rejection. You are either driven to achieve love or avoid rejection. When a child has experienced hurtful rejection a certain number of times, he develops a strong need to avoid this in the future. By deciding (unconsciously) that he is not lovable, he is assuring this outcome. It becomes a rule that helps him avoid rejection: if he is not lovable, then he will make sure that no one gets close enough to him to love him or be loved by him. He can't be rejected if he loves no one and no one loves him. This is perfectly logical to the unconscious mind. Of course, it comes at a high price, as he'll be unable to sustain a long-term, loving relationship. Most negative beliefs have walls around them—even the ones that push you to lose your boundaries. The belief "The other's needs are more important than mine" compels you to merge with other people's needs as you attempt to fulfill them. The belief "I am what I do" submerges your identity into a primary role that you have in life. At the same time that a belief may cause a loss of boundaries, a wall is erected around the belief that seals it off from any experiences except the ones that support it. The belief is much like the fossilized skeleton of a small animal that remains exactly the same through centuries in spite of changing external circumstances.

The word "belief" implies the quality of absoluteness, unchangeability—the truth. It can even have the flavor of religion, wherein the definition of "to believe" is to have a firm religious faith. Self-concepts and world-concepts are other words for beliefs. They both describe the reality of belief: something conceived in the mind, an idea generalized from particular instances concerning the self and/or the world. A self-concept or world-concept is created as a result of a decision you have made about who you are, what you're capable of, and what the world is, based on one experience or an accumulation of experiences.

Self-concepts and world-concepts are not ultimate truths or descriptions of reality, they are subjective associations you have made about yourself and the world driven by your need for safety and pleasure or avoidance of danger and pain. They are ideas that you have created in your mind and therefore can be changed in your mind—you can change your mind! When you develop boundaries around your negative self-concept or world-concept, you allow yourself to be challenged by contrary experiences, thus making room for new learnings to take place. A more accurate and useful word for these ideas you have about yourself and the world is self/world-concept.

You create your self-concepts and world-concepts from the following:

1. Society's rules and definitions.
2. Others' ideas of who and what you are and what the world is.
3. Random associations you make based upon certain experiences.

A rule some societies have is expressed as the cliché, "Children should be seen and not heard." A young girl develops the idea that in order to be "good" she must be quiet and not speak up or express herself. She becomes a quiet, shy person because that cliché planted the seed that became, "I'm shy." Other societies send a different message: thin and angular is beautiful, plump and rounded is unattractive, women are nurturers and men are strong. If you swallow these ideas, you cannot be feminine and strong, masculine and nurturing, or sexy and plump, at least in those societies. A mother keeps telling her daughter how smart she is, or a father criticizes his son for never doing things quite right, or a teacher tells a girl she's having trouble with mathematics because "girls have a natural inclination for literature, not math." When you swallow these ideas, they turn up as self-concepts that you might carry throughout your life.

Another example might be the girl who believes she is tone deaf. As an adolescent, she is told to only mouth the words of a song when her class is putting on a concert. When she sings "Happy Birthday" with her friends, they laugh at her singing. She is told to try out for a speaking-only part rather than a singing part in the school play. These experiences stack up in her mind to the irrefutable reality that she's tone deaf.

Examples of Self-Concepts

I am: open – closed – compassionate – stubborn – a loser – a loner – insecure – dependent – independent – traditional – different – funny – serious – manipulative – loving – unlovable – fragile – strong – a survivor – resilient – rich – poor – successful – a failure – ugly – attractive – sexy – friendly – a money maker – creative – an artist – unworthy – undeserving – a fighter – angry – sensitive – religious – spiritual – clumsy – graceful – shy – uncompromising – a lover – a perfectionist – intellectual – smart – stupid – not enough – bad – good – responsible – evil.

Examples of World-Concepts

The world is/people are: dangerous – selfish – trustworthy – needy – difficult – nurturing – a playground – a puzzle – magical – an opportunity – powerful – hostile – demanding – unpredictable – happy – sad – good – bad – inconsistent – unknowable – irresponsible – ugly – war – destructive – intrusive – wondrous.

To become more aware of your self-concepts and world-concepts, look at the following areas of your life. In each, identify a couple of positive or negative ideas you have about yourself, your capabilities, or the world:

1. Family.
2. Intimate, sexual relationships.
3. Your work or profession—include in this area money, status, and success.
4. Your social life—friends, popularity, acceptance, fun.
5. Your spiritual life—include religion or whatever else means "spiritual" to you.
6. Your health.
7. The self, as in learning, changing, evolution, and creativity.

Let's consider that in your family, you've always been the *peacemaker*; that becomes a strong self-concept. If you're the one who forgets to do certain things, you become *unreliable*. Your flirting is considered cute and is often responded to positively—you become *sexy* or *attractive*. Your high grades scare some boys off, and you become *smart* but not sexy. You get bored in your first couple of jobs, get distracted, and have trouble following through—you're *lazy*. If you keep asking about the criteria for promotion, you're labeled *ambitious*. You live in a large town and are interested in sports and the drama club, so you have two sets of friends and are invited to twice as many parties—you're *popular*. You meditate regularly and are interested in Indian philosophy, so you are *spiritual*. You're a runner and lift weights, so you're *strong*. You have asthma and people treat you a little differently, so you're *delicate*. You've been surrounded by creative people most of your life, and any of your creative endeavors have been warmly received—you're *creative*. No one in your family has ever gone to college, and you see that they don't seem to do much with their lives, so you go in another direction: you go to college and become a *student* and a *learner*.

To further increase awareness of your self-concepts and world-concepts, think of either limiting or particularly positive experiences that are recurring in any one of the above areas, and ask yourself what you are taking for granted about yourself and the situation. "What am I assuming is true about me, my capabilities, or the world?" Have you swallowed whole other people's labels of you or the situation? Perhaps you have accepted as true the ideas about who you are beneath the roles you play or your attributes in some areas of your life.

> Simeon, a 40-year-old pediatrician, was dissatisfied with his work; he knew he was practicing good medicine but something was missing. He was making decent money and his patients were doing well, so what was wrong? He began to look at his professional life through the lens of self-concepts and world-concepts. When he asked himself what he had assumed to be true about his work, he was startled to come up with, "Science is everything." This concept made him shut out anything and everything that did not fit his rather rigid definition of science. He had swallowed this concept and definition from one of his professors in pre-med school when he was an inexperienced and impressionable student. As a result,

he really didn't pay attention to his patients as individuals and certainly was not open to any kind of alternative approaches to children and their health. As Simeon opened up this concept, he became interested in the growing phenomenon of parents who were refusing to have their children vaccinated. Before he had simply dismissed them as irresponsible, but now he began to read up on vaccinations—outside the traditional and accepted scientific literature—and realized that there was another valid point of view. Most importantly, he started to relate on a personal level with his patients, seeing them as unique human beings rather than objects of scientific inquiry. This enriched his day-to-day experience; he was revitalized intellectually by going outside the box of the traditional definition of science and that of his world-concept.

You owe it to yourself to become aware of your self-concepts and world-concepts so you have some choice, rather than allowing them to run your life. Without this choice, you are a victim of your impressionability, vulnerability, and random associations. When you know what your self-concepts and world-concepts are, you can choose to keep them or change them.

Since self-concepts and world-concepts about your identity are not your identity, what role do they play in this identity puzzle? Your identity is your essence, and your most deeply held self-concepts and world-concepts are manifestations of this essence within the environment in which you were born, grew up, and live today. Think of a sunflower, a starburst, or a galaxy: each has a center, surrounded by elements that are dependent on the center yet independent. Connected and separate. At the center of you is your essence (some may call this the soul, spirit, or God; that is an individual choice). Blossoming out from this core are your most important self-concepts and world-concepts. They are the manifestations of your essence. Your essence remains constant and stable, providing a solid anchor for your identity while your self-concepts and world-concepts may expand or contract, depending upon circumstances.

When there are boundaries around your self-concepts and world-concepts, they are shaped and nourished by the way external events interact with your particular strengths and vulnerabilities, allowing growth and flexibility. Negative self-concepts and world-concepts are held in place by walls that prevent any exchange of information. The walls prevent your experiences from having any impact on your self-concepts and world-concepts. Negative self-concepts and world-concepts can be changed by awareness and permeability, by boundaries that expose them to light, air, and space. With boundaries, positive self-concepts and world-concepts develop, adjust, expand, or contract depending on your experiences. For example, you consider yourself a loyal person, and over time, you learn that it's not wise to be loyal to everyone; people have to earn your loyalty. You learn to recognize those people and appreciate the deep satisfaction this quality brings you. In this way, your self-concept is refined and strengthened. In order for a self-concept to remain negative, it must be surrounded by walls. (Negative means extremely limiting in some or all areas of your life.) The walls do not allow external experiences to have any affect on the concept. You believe you are clumsy. You have big feet and hands; whenever you've tried to dance, you step all over your partner's feet, and when drinking from a delicate glass, you always seem to drop it. Of course, with this idea firmly planted in your mind, you expect to be clumsy and break things, and so you do. The walls prevent you from experiencing the grace with which you cast your fishing rod, or climb a tree and chain-saw the top branches, or ride your horse. Without the walls this idea (self-concept) could not survive.

To reshape or fine-tune any of your self-concepts or world-concepts, ask yourself the following questions:

1. "Did I get this idea about myself from the world or from others? If from others, who, specifically?"
2. "Did I get this idea about myself or the world from society's values? Which ones?"
3. "Did I get this idea about myself or the world from experiences? Which ones?"
4. "Is this idea beneficial to me? Do I want to keep it or change it? If yes, change it to what?"

Shining the light of awareness on certain self-concepts and world-concepts is sometimes enough to create boundaries, thus allowing your experiences to affect and begin to shift your concepts. Sometimes not. Sometimes it takes more time for the transformation to take place, but once you become aware of a negative or destructive self-concept or world-concept, it cannot remain the same. Once you've made love, held a bird in your hand, watched the sun rise over the ocean, looked a whale in the eye, or held the hand of a newborn baby, you are forever changed. So too, as walls fall and light and energy are allowed into these negative ideas about yourself, they will never be the same. When there are difficulties transforming the walls into boundaries, remember that those stubborn walls are controlled by a part that is responsible for the value around which the self-concept or world-concept is organized, a part that is waiting to be acknowledged and appreciated. Learn about this part, respect it, communicate with it, and as it learns to trust you, the walls will become boundaries.

> Stella was a choreographer who had the self-concept that she was "damaged goods." This manifested itself in her life as the inability to draw a line and stand up for what she wanted; she would let others influence her unduly or collapse under the pressure of money and time constraints. This affected her finished creative product and kept reinforcing her concept of herself as damaged goods. She became aware of this self-concept and where it came from—her father—but this awareness didn't seem to have any impact. As she became more familiar with the part of her responsible for this self-concept and began to acknowledge him (it was a him), she learned that the part's purpose was to keep her connected to the external, practical world and make a positive impression on others. The part believed that if he allowed Stella to stand up for herself creatively, she would disconnect from the practical world and alienate people. If he gave up the walls around the self-concept of damaged goods and let her experiences affect it, he feared he would have no more purpose and would cease to exist. With time and further communication in which his purpose was acknowledged and honored, he realized that his purpose could be better served with boundaries. This would enable him to choose when Stella must stick to her guns and when she should compromise. Choice protected her better than constant compliance. This work allowed Stella to gradually shift her self-concept from "I'm damaged goods" to "I'm an artist."

It is comforting and centering to have a concrete experience of your identity. The following suggestions are helpful in accomplishing this objective:

1. Through your unconscious mind, find a name for your essence that is organic and originates in your gut.
2. Identify your most fundamental self-concepts and world-concepts.
3. Be sure there are boundaries around these concepts so that the energy flow from your essence to these self-concepts and world-concepts and back to your essence is uninterrupted.

It is important to name your essence, because the name separates it from the complexity of the rest of you. It provides a handle that makes it easier to connect to your essential beingness. The name makes concrete an intangible metaphor and centers you, providing a foundation for self-esteem. The following Identity Ritual will help you to realize these suggestions.

Identity Ritual

You can do this alone or with someone you trust. The goal of this ritual is to create an open, free channel to your unconscious mind. When a word emerges from your unconscious as a result of this ritual, it becomes a representation of a complete mind–body experience rather than an intellectual label that has little meaning. Words that represent self-concepts and world-concepts are either negative or positive: loving, smart, clumsy, fair, visible, nonexistent, responsible, loser, and so on. Words that represent essence are neither negative nor positive: they represent beingness; something that simply is, like energy, light, green grass, wind, woman, alive, spirit, space, tree, nature, and so on.

> If you do this alone, you need a tape-recorder and a quiet place where you'll be undisturbed. Begin by getting comfortable, relaxing, meditating, or just being quiet. Turn on the recorder. After a few moments, ask yourself out loud, "And who am I?" Answer in two words or less. Use a quiet, low tonality and slow tempo. Trust the first impulse, the first response that comes—and remember that it doesn't have to make cognitive sense! This is not an intellectual

exercise. Keep repeating this question and answering until you no longer have to ask the question. You'll slip into a rhythm and a different pace from your ordinary consciousness. You'll come up with more and more words, "And I am …" Keep repeating, "and I am …" The process of connecting to the unconscious mind is like peeling an onion; you uncover one layer at a time gently, carefully, and persistently. Repetition that is respectful and gentle is the secret to reaching the unconscious. After 20 to 30 minutes of this, listen to the tape, and you'll notice that you began to repeat some words, and gradually you'll keep going back to one, two, or three words. Write these down, staying as connected to your unconscious as possible. Turn on the recorder again, sit quietly, and repeat those words, "And I am …" and ask again "And who am I?" Eventually, you will find the word that connects you to your essence. You will recognize it.

All of the above can apply when doing this ritual with someone else. The other person acts as the guide, and asks the question in a quiet, gentle, slow voice, "And who are you?" over and over again, writing down your answers (of course, there is no need for a tape recorder). From time to time, your guide will repeat back to you your answers, "And you are …" until you have found the word. The entire ritual must be slow, relaxed, and not attached to any outcome.

What's important is not whether you find the right word, but whether it's the obvious word to you. You'll cripple your connection to your unconscious if you worry about "getting it right."

This word puts boundaries around your essence, and is the core of your identity.

> Tina did this ritual with a guide and came up with words such as mother, caring, angry, intelligent, compassionate, teacher, friend, daughter, a leader, energy, connected, oceans, woman, growing, angry, arrogant, impatient, a hermit, shy, caring, woman, mother, sensual, caring, energy, woman, lover, woman, mother, woman, woman, woman, woman! This is a compressed version that, in real clock time, took well over 30 minutes. Tina reported that this word "woman" had tremendous meaning for her now. Before the ritual, she knew she was a woman, and she thought she knew what it

meant. Having gone through the ritual, this word "woman" had a very deep, personal, and profound meaning. She felt connected to it in a different way; now the word defined her in all her many complexities and faces, honoring her uniqueness and connecting her to the cosmos. She had connected her experience of her whole self to a word. She was moved, and it made real and knowable her identity. Knowing who you are centers and grounds you and strengthens the foundation of your evolution and self-esteem.

Identity Meditation

Imagine a place in your body where you want to put your essence and a sensation connected to it. Create an image of the word defining your essence and a voice to say the word. Put these all together to form a multisensory experience of your essence. For example: "light" said with a high, drawn-out, resonant voice, accompanied by an image of the white foam at the crest of an ocean wave, and a cool expanding sensation in and around your head. Practice this until it becomes familiar and easy to imagine and experience. Identify four to six of your most important self-concepts and world-concepts. Be sure that all are positive with boundaries; give each a one-word name. The word of your essence and your self-concepts and world-concept create the image of a flower: essence is the center and the self-concepts and world-concepts are the petals connected to yet separate from the center. Allow yourself to connect with the experience of each self-concept and world-concept as fully as possible. Take your time and dream the dream of each one. Now, sitting quietly, hear, see, and feel your essence, and imagine it reaching out and connecting to each of your self-concepts and world-concepts. There is a harmonious flow of energy from your essence to each and back to your essence.

Thus, your identity is your essential beingness expressed through your ideas of self and the world. These ideas can change during different phases of your life and circumstances while your essence remains constant. This constancy strengthens your experience of yourself as a process and as a separate unique individual, supporting your awareness of and capacity for creating and maintaining boundaries. As you identify your self-concepts and world-concepts, you are separating them from the dogma of beliefs and connecting them to your experiences and to your essence. With boundaries, they are no longer written in stone, blocking the flow of energy from your essence to external manifestation. Your identity is no longer an intellectual, superficial idea or a mushy, undifferentiated feeling. It is now something made more tangible that connects your mind, heart, body, and soul.

Everyone has an identity. The important question is how you define yourself and how this definition serves you or not. Is the name you give yourself, the word you call yourself a dead end, a prison, or a beginning—a starburst?

Once upon a time, there was a young woman named Melody. She had recently completed her very long and intensive training to become a *good witch*. She was waiting, somewhat impatiently, to be called for her testing in order to be certified as a *good witch* by the Council of Elders of the Good Witches of the World.

Finally, she was summoned to appear before this council. She was nervous but even more excited, and so when she came before them, she immediately began to ask, "What do I have to do to be certified? Tell me what my test is. What do you want to know? How can I demonstrate my abilities?"

The members of the Council of Elders simply smiled benignly at her while she became more and more frustrated. She continued to ask them what she had to do to prove her worthiness, and they continued to smile until in a flash of light, they magically disappeared.

Melody fell into a deep sleep, and when she awoke, she found herself in a new and strange world. She was annoyed with the lack of answers from the Council of Elders, but curiosity got the better of her, and she began to explore this new world. She discovered she was in Rome during the first century and, as she got to know the city and the people, she realized there was great need for her skills and magic. She comforted and healed many—both physically and emotionally—made many friends, fell in love, and prospered in her relationships.

One morning, upon awakening, one of the elders of the Council of Elders of the Good Witches of the World was beside her bed. Melody began to ask her about her testing and certification, but the elder held out her hand and led her to a great and beautifully carved wooden door. As they passed through and the door closed behind them, Melody realized it was the door to her world. She became very angry, shouting, "No, I don't want to leave yet. I have friends I don't want to leave. I have work yet to finish. Why are you doing this?" By then the elder had disappeared, and Melody continued for a while to bang on the door and try to open it. It was no use, and finally she fell into a deep sleep. When she awoke, she began to explore this new world and found herself in Europe during the Middle Ages. Gradually, she realized that many people here in this world needed her magic—there was much pain and suffering here. She made new friends and loves, and she understood that those she had left behind in her old world were in some way still with her. Each one who had been important to her had marked her—her thinking, her actions, her heart—and so she carried them with her in this new world. Melody worked and learned and loved, and one day when she woke, an elder was beside her bed. She didn't want to leave her world but knew she must and so followed the elder through the great carved door. Again she tried to get the elder to tell her when she would be certified, what was her testing, what this was all about. But the elder simply smiled and disappeared. Melody was very sad to leave her world, but knew she couldn't change the will of the elders. She cried for her lost world, slept, and awoke to explore her new world—America in the twentieth century. There was much work for her in this chaotic and troubled world, and she was comforted by the knowledge that she brought with her from her old worlds, all her experience and learnings—and something special from all those important people who had touched her life.

One day when Melody woke up, she knew this was the day she must leave this world and follow the call to her next world. Although sad to leave this world, she knew that she brought everything important with her. As she passed through the carved door, she paused to bid that world farewell and, as she turned toward her new world, her face was lit with a inner glow of excitement and anticipation of what new learnings and what new loves awaited her. At that moment, the elder of the Council of Good Witches of the World appeared, smiled and as she took Melody's hand she said, "Welcome to the Council of the Good Witches of the World."

At last Melody understood what testing truly meant. Each day that she learned and loved was a success, and so she laughed, her face glowing with tears of happiness.

Chapter X

Boundaries and Self-Esteem

Self-esteem is defined as your relationship with yourself. This chapter describes how either the presence or the distortion of boundaries affects the possibility of a positive, functioning relationship with yourself. This point is explored in depth in several important areas: acceptance versus attachment, appropriate and inappropriate emotions, idealized self, expectations, and the dynamics of change. These areas are the most critical in either developing and supporting self-esteem or eroding and crippling self-esteem.

Who are your best friends? How do you talk to them, think about them, feel about them? If they disappoint you or make a mistake, do you forsake your friendship? You do your best to care for them when they are in need, and seek their comfort and assistance when you are hurting. You may get angry with them at times, but mostly you are kind, respectful, and patient. You understand that they are human and, as such, imperfect with weaknesses and shortcomings. In your eyes, their strengths and virtues are what is essential. You appreciate the whole person of your dearest friends, and you nurture your relationship with them.

What is your relationship with yourself? Are you kind, respectful, patient, and appreciative? Self-esteem is not loving yourself, it is not self-confidence; it is your relationship with yourself. It is the most important relationship you will ever have, as all other relationships are built on it. Self-esteem rests on a three-legged stool of boundaries, nonpolar thinking, and identity, all of which are necessary for self-esteem to exist. When you are separate from all else *and* connected to the world around you, you can think in a nonjudgmental way and have a solid sense of your identity.

Boundaries enable development of a self; identity incorporates your values and gives meaning to this self; and nonpolar thinking allows you to relate to yourself without judgment.

Acceptance

When you can deliberately think in a nonjudgmental way, making the step to acceptance is much easier. Acceptance is the foundation of self-esteem and the foundation of a functional relationship with yourself. (I speak of acceptance in terms of "receiving," rather than in the more common meaning of approval.) To accept is to receive; no conditions can be attached. When you receive, you are open, available, and vulnerable, not defensive or judgmental. To have self-esteem, you must be able to accept, to receive who you are at that moment, without approval or judgment. In order to do this, you must be able to make a distinction (boundaries) between your entire being and your behaviors, thoughts, or feelings at a moment in time. In other words, being aware that you were mean to your friend, dishonest with your colleague, or selfish and self-centered with your partner, and acknowledging that that behavior is something you need to change, is the first step toward a positive relationship with yourself. The second step is doing this without judging yourself as a mean, dishonest, or selfish person. Condemning yourself—feeling like you're bad, evil, useless, or no good—is not a productive place from which to learn and change. You are not your behavior, your thoughts, or your feelings. You are human, which means being imperfect. You will make mistakes, behave in ways that are not always kind, think badly of others, and experience jealousy, envy, or hatred toward others. Think of these as challenges and opportunities to grow. To be aware of your shortcomings, accepting them, learning from them, and changing something about yourself is precisely how you evolve. Acceptance is not an excuse to continue to be hurtful to others or destructive to yourself; nor does hating yourself help you to be a kinder, better person.

Fred is 35 years old and has a complicated relationship with his father. As a teenager, he yelled at his father and said some very nasty things to him. When he got really upset, he would tell him he wished he were dead! Today, Fred often loses boundaries between the past and the present when he and his father have a disagreement. He feels guilty and hates himself for being a "bad" son. The worse he feels about himself, the less control he has over his behavior and what he says to his father. He loves his father, but he hates himself so much that as soon as he gets a little bit impatient with his father, he escalates to a nasty, full-blown attack on him. Then, of course, he feels even worse about himself, and the cycle continues. It's as though he's proving what a miserable person he is. The collapse of boundaries between Fred's behavior and his identity around his father makes him feel like a "bad" son. This results in walls between his love for his father and his father. When he feels irritation with his father, he collapses into the irritation; it escalates into rage, and he has no access to his love for him. Fred has attached his identity to his behavior. When he can accept his behavior without telling himself that he's a bad son, he can stay connected to his love for his father and begin to change his behavior. Boundaries would help him see his father as a separate person whom he loves, rather than an extension of his "bad" self.

Consider the difference between *acceptance* and *attachment*. Acceptance is to receive, while attachment is to bind together; with acceptance there are boundary distinctions between identity and behavior. Attachment has no boundaries. It binds together like a "super glue" with no space between, certainly no distinctions. It compels you to become one with another person, idea, a job, or thing. To be attached to someone or something can be beautiful as long as you are aware and freely choose to do so for a certain amount of time. To be automatically and habitually attached to a philosophy, religion, ideology, or person means to give up yourself as a separate individual. Attachment can be dangerous or destructive, because you no longer have free choice or take responsibility for yourself and your actions. When you are driven by attachment, you annihilate self-esteem. There is no separate self with whom to relate.

There was once a famous guru to whom people from all over the world came to study. One day, a woman came and asked to learn from his wisdom. He answered her thus: "You must cut off your long beautiful hair before you can learn with me." She asked why, and he simply told her the same thing, "First you must cut off your hair." She argued that learning with him had nothing to do with her hair. She continued to fight, she begged, pleaded, threatened, and reasoned—all to no avail. Finally, after a very long time, she cut her hair. It was then that she had the inner space and freedom to truly learn about herself. On another day, another woman came to learn from the guru. She also had long, beautiful hair, and when he asked her to cut off her hair, she replied, "Do you have a scissors? I will do it now!" The guru said to her, "No, there is no need for you to cut your hair at all."

Emotions

Your self-esteem is fueled by your emotions. However, emotions don't really exist. An emotion is an idea or thought, or something you perceive externally with one of your five senses that is associated with a physical sensation. You then label this with a word that you call an *emotion*. What we call emotions are powerful; they compel and drive all of us throughout our lives! The challenge of emotions is threefold:

1. Be aware of what emotion you're feeling when you're feeling it. (This can only be done by becoming sensitive to and tuned in to your body, learning the language of your body).
2. The free choice to express (externalize verbally and non-verbally) your emotions in a timely way.
3. Maintain boundaries between past emotions and present emotions.

Appropriate and Inappropriate Emotions

Emotions are appropriate or inappropriate. This is not labeling emotions as good or bad, right or wrong but distinguishing emotions that either *match* the circumstances of a situation (appropriate) or emotions that do not match the circumstances of a situation (inappropriate). A parent who experiences anxiety when his child goes off to her first day of school is having an appropriate emotion. However, if after six months he continues to experience the same level of anxiety each time his daughter leaves for school, I would say that is an inappropriate emotion. The emotion does not match the circumstances of the situation. The way that you handle and respond to these inappropriate emotions will be determined by your self-esteem and will in turn affect your self-esteem. An inappropriate emotion is not wrong; rather it is an opportunity to become more aware of what is going on in your life. Inappropriate emotions are like physical symptoms, especially the ones that recur frequently. They are important messages about you and your life. When you repeatedly experience an inappropriate emotion, accept it. Receive the emotion and allow yourself to feel it. Do not run away from it with sex, alcohol, or drugs, by denying it, by walling it off, or trying to explain it away. Feel it and recognize that it is an inappropriate emotion for the circumstances. Acknowledge that it is a message about your life, and begin to explore what that message could be! You may immediately become aware of what that is or it could remain hidden in your unconscious. Be patient with yourself. Feel the emotion and keep reminding yourself that it is a message. Instead of trying to get rid of it because it is uncomfortable or to understand the reasons for it, ask yourself, "What could this emotion be trying to tell me about my life?" Trust me, the message *will* make itself known to you when you are open to the possibility. While the message of any inappropriate emotion is individual and personal, there are universal messages under certain emotions. These are some examples:

- Guilt—a message that you have violated your own values and standards.
- Depression—a message that you need to change something in your life.
- Envy—a message that you want something.
- Anger—a message that you have to stop the abuse from some part of your external or internal world.
- Inadequacy—a message there is an opportunity to learn.
- Fear—a challenge to determine whether you can do something about a situation or not—if you can, do it; if you can't, accept that there's nothing more you can do.
- Procrastination—a message that either you don't know how to do something or you don't want to do something.
- Regret—a message that you can learn to do something better or different the next time.
- Anxiety—a message that you need to create a goal for yourself.
- Disappointment—a message that you have to change your expectations.
- Frustration—a message about finding other options to accomplish something.
- Hopeless—a message to let go of something.

Paula was chronically late for everything! She was single, attractive, and had a great job as an assistant producer for a big television station. She called herself "The Great Procrastinator!" She procrastinated when it was time to leave for work, writing her reports, getting to important meetings, paying her bills, returning phone calls—she procrastinated over nearly everything she was supposed to do. She kept telling herself she should leave the house earlier for work, start on her reports weeks before they were due, and pay her bills when they came in, but she never did. There was always something else that got her attention. Her life became very stressful, and she was constantly on the edge of disaster. Her mortgage canceled, bosses angry, getting fired, friends upset—her world was becoming more and more chaotic. Somehow she always seemed to pull it off and avoid disaster, but it was taking a toll on her emotional and physical health. She was nervous, had headaches, beat herself up a lot, and was certainly not enjoying any of her successes or her life! As we worked together, she began to recognize that she didn't want to be a TV producer and live in a big city. She didn't want to go to work every day in a large office building with lots of people and electronics. She really wanted to work outdoors, away from people. Paula is now a park ranger in the Rocky Mountains and she no longer procrastinates. She even pays her bills on time!

There are certain emotions you like and enjoy feeling; they bring satisfaction and fulfillment. There are others that recur frequently that you don't like; you dread them and want to avoid them. Those are the emotions you probably need to feel. The recurring inappropriate emotions are your teachers. They are telling you something about your life, and when you learn from them you are relating to yourself in a way that is positive, respectful, and dynamic.

Idealized Self

When you regard yourself as worthy and of value, you have self-esteem—this comes out of a respectful relationship with yourself. One of the most seductive traps you can fall into, one that is guaranteed to destroy self-esteem, is your idealized self. It's wonderful to have an ideal self—it provides goals and motivates you to grow and evolve. How could this be bad? It becomes negative when there are no boundaries between your ideal self and your present self, as occurs when your present and idealized self reside in the same time frame. When you keep comparing your present self with your ideal self in the same moment of time, you will always come up short. Your present self is not supposed to be the same as your ideal self. It's your "ideal" self! So how can it be good to have an ideal self? When you put your ideal self in the future, not the present, the ideal self becomes something to move toward and reach for, an ideal rather than the present standard against which you measure yourself now. As long as your ideal self is in the future, separate from but connected to the present, it will serve as a goal that motivates you now.

> Krista was 25 years old, a very talented pianist, and very miserable. She was finding it impossible to audition for jobs; her teacher and colleagues recommended her, but she would become so negative about her abilities and talent that she became paralyzed. This became an insidious cycle, and she became increasingly miserable. She had always had high standards for herself and others. These standards had guided her to one of the most renowned piano teachers in the world. This teacher accepted Krista because of her extraordinary talent, but Krista was not developing. She needed to work and get experience, but she lost all self-confidence when the time came to audition. Krista knew exactly how she should play at auditions and had created an idealized audition-playing self. This ideal self was based on all the greatest players in the world plus Krista's perfectionist standards. Every time she prepared for an audition, she compared herself with this ideal—in the present, saying, "I should already be playing like this." Of course Krista was not up to her idealized self at that moment, because it represented a future potential. She felt bad about herself, judged and criticized herself until she lost all belief in her talent. Normally, this idealized self kept Krista practicing and improving because it motivated her. Except, when she was preparing for an audition, this ideal self was right in her face, representing how she "should" be playing "now! That paralyzed her.

I taught Krista to imagine that she was traveling on a road through life and how the road ahead was her future. The following exercise helped her. The present is the immediate space around you, while the future is somewhere ahead of you and the past is behind you—the road you've already traveled. Although you can't know the content of your future, you do have images and feelings about the future, possibilities both positive and negative. These future "memories" are somehow different from your past memories, not just in their content but how they look: bigger, smaller, darker or lighter, more focused or less, framed or soft-edged, color or black and white. You know the difference between something you know because you've actually *experienced* it and something you *want* to happen, something you wish for in the future. Your dream can seem very vivid and real, but still you know it hasn't happened yet. That's because your mind represents the future differently from the present and the past. Most of the time, your mind makes boundaries between the different time frames. The ideal self is an exception.

> Together Krista and I took her idealized self, who she liked and wanted to keep (it represented important values) and put that image into her future. We put it on the road ahead of her—not too close or too far—made the image slightly out of focus, large, and soft-edged. This type of image matched other things she knew were in her future and hadn't experienced yet: moving to a new apartment, visiting a friend in Boston next month, and going to Paris to study. Krista was comforted by keeping her ideal self and very excited by putting it in the future. Now when she compared her present playing for an audition to her idealized playing, she could appreciate what she was doing well now and how she was moving toward her future goal. She immediately felt better about herself and her present skills, and was more determined than ever to achieve her ideal—in the future. Of course, when she actually begins to get close to her goal, she will readjust her ideal to encompass higher and more subtle standards that she can't yet even imagine.

Without dreams to look forward to, life would be dull; dreams help you reach for the stars. Practice your boundary skills with the three different time frames: past, present, and future. It is critical for your self-esteem to keep these separate *and* connected.

Expectations

A bit of chaos is exciting and stimulates creativity. Too much chaos drives you mad, just as too much certainty constrains and stifles you. However, human beings need some amount of certainty: you need to know the sidewalk will still be there the next time you walk out your front door, that your house will be standing when you go home, and that the sun will rise tomorrow morning. A certain amount of predictability is necessary to sustain sanity. Out of this necessity you build your expectations. To have some structure and coherency in your life, you have to be able to expect some things to remain constant: you learn to expect the lights will go on when you flip the switch or your shoes to fit when you put them on—you expect the fundamentals of your life to stay in place. From those mundane but basic expectations, you learn to anticipate other events, like your friend meeting you at the time she said she would, being treated respectfully by your boss at work, or your wife sharing her day with you. Expectations aren't bad or destructive—they're natural, but when they become walled off from your actual experience, they become another trap into which your self-esteem can be twisted out of shape.

Misguided expectations are created out of a loss of boundaries between your wishes or hopes and what you come to expect. When you hope for something hard enough, you may begin to expect it; it's no longer a dream or wish but an expectation that something will or should actually happen. It's great to wish or hope for something, but when the reality proves to be very different over and over again, it's time to adjust your expectations by taking reality into consideration. When you want something very badly, the expectation becomes so familiar that it gets walled off from reality. Now it's an expectation that's locked in—and you may not even realize it. You just know you're continually disappointed that your friend is never on time for your meetings. You keep expecting her to be on time because *you* would be, and then you either get angry and fight with her or begin to question your own worth as a friend. For you it's important to be punctual when you've agreed to meet someone at a certain time. When you put that value onto your friend (loss of boundaries), you expect her to be on time. Even though she's consistently late, you keep holding onto an expectation that is contrary to the reality: her repeated lateness (walls).

You keep feeling insulted, disappointed, or worthless and you sulk or fight with your friend. When you do meet, it isn't enjoyable for either of you, or it may end up being pleasant but it takes a lot of recrimination and resentment to get to that point. In any case, you're not feeling very good about yourself.

> Felice was a successful investment banker with a high-level executive position in a small investment firm. Her immediate bosses were the partner-owners of the company, which had offices in several major cities in Europe and the U.S. She ran the London office, and in the five years she had been with the company, she tripled that office's net profit. She was hard-working, innovative, and very smart. She knew the business and was good at what she did. Her two bosses would repeatedly get angry over small details, lose their temper, and yell at her. As time went by, she felt worse and worse: she was angry at them, questioned herself, and her own value. Felice had the expectation that her bosses would treat her respectfully and behave with professionalism because if she had been the boss, she would behave that way. In spite of the reality, she held onto her expectation because it represented "the right thing to do." She kept expecting her bosses to change and control themselves—and when they didn't she became more upset, began to doubt herself, beat herself up because she stayed in the situation, and gradually her self-confidence was being worn down.

When your reality matches your expectations, you feel comforted and safe. You feel vindicated or reassured that you have some control over your life. When your reality doesn't match your expectations, you might sometimes be surprised and delighted, but many times you feel frustrated and upset.

When you get into the same type of situation over and over again where you come away frustrated or disappointed, ask yourself what were your expectations going into that situation. You must become aware of what your expectation is and then separate it from the reality of what actually happens. Compare your expectation and the reality, and consider your choices. You can:

1. Adjust your expectation according to the reality. You're creating boundaries between the two, allowing the information in the reality to permeate and influence the expectation.

2. Keep your expectation as it is and get out of the reality situation (in this case, your expectations influence your reality).

3. Keep your expectation the same and stay in the same situation. At least now you can choose to enjoy being frustrated or disappointed!

When meeting a friend who is always late you can:

1. Change your expectation that she will be on time—given the reality—and expect her to be late, preparing yourself by bringing along some paperwork or a good book to enjoy while you wait for her. This could actually help you carve out some extra time for yourself in your busy day. When she finally arrives, you can begin to enjoy her company immediately.

2. Decide that the value you have built your expectation on is so important that you cannot tolerate your friend's blatant disregard for it, and you can choose not to have this person any longer in your life. It's just not worth it. Here again you are separating the expectation from the reality and connecting them by allowing the expectation to influence the reality.

3. Keep everything the same and continue to do as you always have. In this case, you must take responsibility for your own frustration and perhaps even choose to enjoy it!

When Felice became conscious of her expectations about her bosses and their behavior, she looked at the reality and realized how deeply they violated her values. She could no longer maintain her expectations so she changed them to match the reality, and since that reality was unacceptable to her, the decision to leave was easy. During the six months she took to train her replacement, prepare her office for her departure (her values), and find another job, her bosses' unprofessional behavior no longer affected her self-confidence. Previously, Felice had kept herself in denial of her bosses' true nature by holding on to her expectations and keeping them totally separate (walls) from the reality. Once she created some permeability between the two, her expectations changed and she knew she had to change the reality. Her bosses could no longer violate or disappoint her. She was able to recognize them for who they were and not expect anything different.

In any recurring difficult situation, take a look at your expectations, be aware of what specifically you expect, and compare that with the reality. Ask yourself, "Given the reality, do I want to change my expectations so that I feel better about myself and the situation?" Or, "Given my expectations and the values represented by them, do I need to change the reality?" Or, "Do I want to keep everything the same and continue to be upset and disappointed?"

I believe people are capable of changing. Consider any of your friends and look at how they are at 45 compared to how they were at 20. Look back at who you were 25 years ago and consider how much you have changed. Not everyone changes, but I think everyone is capable of change. Your essence remains constant while the way you manifest this essence changes. I'm reminded of my children who are now in their thirties and forties. In some essential way, I recognize the newborn in the adult each has become. When I looked at each as he or she took their first breath, I saw in some inexplicable way who they were to become, and yet each has changed and grown in so many ways over the years. Yes, people do change, and how that change takes place, the anatomy of change, is fascinating to consider. Knowing you can change, knowing you have the ability to achieve your intended change—large and significant or small and mundane—empowers you and strengthens your self-esteem.

Erickson's Principles of Change

The clearest and most helpful principles that describe how change happens were developed by Dr. Milton Erickson. According to Erickson, at least one of the following three principles must be present whenever change occurs in human behavior, thinking, or feeling.

1. *The ability to change perspective.* I have discussed this in previous chapters but not specifically in the context of change. "I never thought about it in that way." "Look at this from my point of view." "If I were you, I'd be upset also." "Suddenly I could see where she was coming from." These are all cliché phrases

that take on new meaning when you consider them through the lens of changing perspective. "Perspective is a matter of life and death. One point perspective ... is a dead view, a mechanical view, the view of an unmoving, unblinking eye. We're 3-D creatures." ("David Hockney and Friends," Mathew Garewitsch, *Smithsonian Magazine*, August 2006.)

Look at the world through someone else's eyes, hear conversation through someone else's ears, allow yourself to identify with someone else's emotions—all these shifts in perspective immeasurably broaden your view and understanding of the world. You get more information, new and different types of information, while keeping intact your sense of self through maintaining your boundaries. You can change your perspective not only by stepping into someone else's shoes but also by simply changing your position in space. Consider that you are at the center of your personal experience of space. Imagine that you could look at yourself and your situation from a different angle: from above yourself, from beside yourself, in front, and behind yourself. There are infinite possibilities: you can describe a 360-degree circle around yourself—but that's just two-dimensional, now make it three-dimensional! There are infinite points from which to view your situation, and every shift gives you a little more or different information, much like a hologram. Imagine that you're 5 years old again and that you're standing on the ground, surrounded by adults, a car, trees, and some tables and chairs. Let your now self be in the body of your 5-year-old self. How do the people look to you? How do the car, trees, and table look? Now imagine that your father or one of your relatives hoists you up on his shoulders and takes you for a walk. Suddenly you're looking directly into your aunt's eyes, you can see the top of the car, and you're looking down at the table and chairs. You're even looking down at your cousins and friends who are close to your age. There's one cousin who's 8 years old and a bit of a bully; he doesn't look so tough from high above, looking down at him!

There are other ways to change your perspective. You can pay more attention to what you see, what you hear, or what you physically sense in your body. You can consider the details or the larger aspects of a situation. You can attend to how things are the same or different or how things would look from the past or the future. The more aware you are of the possibilities, and the more skilled you become at doing them, the easier it is to change—when you really want to!

Remember an important change that you made in your life. Study it to discover what shift in perspective helped you make that change. Look at some small change you made in the last year—what was the change in perspective?

> Henry, who Silas thought was a friend (even though people had warned him not to trust him), had left the room he was renting in Silas' house owing two months rent and some of the electric and heat bills. On top of that, Henry would tell Silas that he was going to give him the money and then never show up or call. This went on for a month. Silas felt used and betrayed. He had helped Henry get a promotion at work and even introduced him to his girlfriend. Silas became obsessed with this betrayal; he thought about it constantly. He was stressed out, losing sleep, and becoming angry at the world. One day he realized that he was allowing Henry to run his life; he was neglecting his work and friends. He stepped back from the situation and considered this incident in the context of his whole life. Henry became a blip on the screen! Silas began to understand that he had important things he wanted to do with his life, and Henry was an unfortunate detail—and not worth so much energy! He changed his perspective from concentrating on a single detail—Henry—to the larger picture of his entire life, both present and future.

Think of what a difference it would make to jump into the future and look back at yourself today! Maybe you're procrastinating about writing that speech you have to make next month or putting off cleaning the house. Go into the future to a point in time after you do what you're avoiding. The situation looks and feels different, doesn't it?

When I get nervous about flying overseas, I begin to make pictures in my head of the plane landing, see myself getting into the car that takes me to the hotel I'm staying at or back home, and returning to my house and my hounds. This always calms me down. I'm shifting my perspective from talking to myself about the dangers of flying and feeling anxious to seeing my arrival.

A couple of times a week, take about five minutes and practice some of the following ways to shift perspective. Pick simple, mundane situations, rather than ones that are highly difficult or traumatic:

- See yourself from behind, in front of, beside, or above yourself, as though your eyes were behind the lens of a camera focused on yourself.
- Hear your voice and words.
- Step back and see and hear the present situation as a small detail on the large screen of your whole life.
- Step inside yourself; connect with your body and become aware of all five senses.
- Imagine it's a day, a week, a month, a year, five years, or fifty years in the future—and you're remembering this situation.
- Pretend that you're on the moon looking down at yourself.
- Imagine your situation through someone else's eyes and ears.
- Create your own ways to change your perspective.

2. *The ability to experience the future.* You know what the word *future* means: it describes tomorrow, next week, next month, next year, five, ten, twenty, or a hundred years from now. It is one of the ways we divide up time: there's the past frame, the present frame, and the future frame. But do you experience in your whole being what the future really means? It is the time that hasn't happened yet and that implies that anything can happen. The future is unknowable; it is different from the now and from the past. There are many constants in life, things that remain the same over time. The sun continues to rise and set, your home still stands, your partner is there every morning—until that day when even one of the most constant elements of your life may change unexpectedly. The essence of the future is difference, the time frame where anything is possible. The past is set. It has been "fired in the kiln of time." You can reinterpret its meaning, change the effect it may have on your present life, or make a different decision about yourself and the world based upon your past, but the stepping stones are immutable.

The present is the most real element of life and yet it is ephemeral. It cannot be captured. The moment you try, it becomes the past. Even as I write these very words, the present slips into the past. The future is open space, is the blank page, the untouched canvas, the silence before the symphony. Milton Erickson likened the future to the light that beckons in the darkness. As long as you experience the future as being different from the past or present, you have unlimited possibilities. You can learn, change, resolve problems, achieve your goals, do things differently, and embrace your potential.

When you have the sense that your present condition is going to go on forever or that tomorrow will be the same as yesterday, you're not experiencing the future. You'll get very depressed, disorganized, stuck in guilt or regret, procrastinate, or be unmotivated or hopeless. Change depends on your ability to experience the future and know that you always have the possibilities of next time. Experiencing the future as different from the past and present supports and strengthens your self-esteem.

> One winter, the temperature fell below freezing—in the single digits—for six weeks straight. I had 30 rose bushes that I had mulched carefully in the fall. I love my rose bushes and have had splendid luck with them. I believe when a rose bush likes where it is, it will grow and make lots of beautiful flowers and be hardy through the spring, summer, and fall. Most of my roses liked the home I gave them. However, the spring after that horribly cold winter, I lost 20 of my precious roses. They were as dead as a doornail! My roses were a vital part of my gardening, and I was devastated—I seriously considered not growing roses anymore! I couldn't understand it and felt like giving up. Then I began to imagine next summer without my roses—how empty and barren it felt. Upon rereading some of my gardening books, I focused on the sentence: "In cold winter climates, when planting your rose bush, bury the crown several inches underground." I realized that I had assumed the person planting my roses would do this, but I had never specifically told her to do so. She was not an expert on roses. I bought 12 new rose bushes and carefully instructed the person helping me to plant them deep. The next winters have not been quite as cold, but they've been cold enough. My roses are surviving into the spring, and they bloom with great enthusiasm.

My sense of the future—and the opportunity to learn and do things differently—enabled me to start over with my roses. There were other springs and summers to experience the luxury and elegance of my roses and other winters to survive by trying something different.

3. *The ability to laugh at oneself.* Erickson's third principle of change is having a sense of humor about yourself. This is finding the humor in something you did, thought, or felt. It is not deprecating yourself or putting yourself down but rather truly accepting and appreciating yourself *and* being able to laugh at yourself.

I'm very proud of my daughter for many reasons, but one of the most important is her independence and her ability to stand up for herself. When she was a teenager and stood up for herself during spirited discussions we were having, I was not very happy about this quality at that moment! However, with a little time and distance, I could look back at specific events and laugh at myself. As a matter of fact, I've used this story many times in my classes! Remember times when you were upset about something and the world seemed to revolve around you and your feelings? It seemed to consume you, but after some time you could actually laugh about your stubbornness or self-righteousness. Even in the moment, you can sometimes appreciate the irony or absurdity of your position or behavior. Having a sense of humor about yourself means that you don't have to take yourself so seriously all the time. You have the right to be serious about some things, but to take yourself seriously all the time means you are suffering from "center of the universe" syndrome! When you were a child, you were and deserved to be the center of the universe. Now that you're grown up, you are no longer the center of the universe! Humor leavens the bread of our existence—it helps put things in perspective, to define what is really important and what seems important in the moment but is actually trivial or silly. You can feel worthy, be silly, ridiculous and be amused. Change often comes when you're able to laugh. My youngest son, bless him, and I were having a disagreement about my political opinions. He got very upset and stalked out. When I saw him the next day, we were talking about other things and suddenly he looked at me and said, "Boy, did I act like a pompous ass yesterday," and he started to laugh and do a funny imitation of himself being a pompous ass! We both had a good laugh together.

Self-esteem means finding yourself worthy of being here in this world and deriving satisfaction from your interactions. A part of that worthiness and satisfaction is becoming aware of your mission in this life. What is your vision? What are you meant to do, to learn, to be? What is your personal quest? It could be simply the quest to discover your mission. It could be to make a difference, to serve others, to touch your own potential, or nature, or … Your mission is like a huge frame you put around your life, not to limit it but to create the large picture of which the individual events are only parts that make up the whole, that give your life perspective and meaning. Meaning is often not earth-shattering but simple, even mundane. "Art's subject is the human clay." (*Letter to Lord Byron* by W. H. Auden, English poet, 1907–1973).

Each person's life is a work of art. Each simple, everyday action celebrates the meaning of life. Washing the dishes, the warm water, the gleam of a clean glass, the sense of accomplishment, the joy of having dishes and warm water, and above all, being alive and able to do this, and so much more according to his/her meanings.

Personal Mission Meditation

There are four systems within you: the physical, the mental, the emotional, and the spiritual, and five external systems within which you interact: intimate (family and sexual), work, the social, the community, and the global (or perhaps cosmic). How all these systems interact is your personal ecology.

Meditate on each system in turn and ask yourself, "What do I want?" and "What will getting it do for me?" within each specific system. For example, "What do I want in my emotional life?" or "What do I want in my intimate life?" Repeat these questions until you access a large concept that feels congruent for each system. Once you can name nine goals, repeat them to yourself. "And physically I want …"; "And emotionally I want …"; "And in my intimate family and/or sexual life I want …" Continue until you have repeated the nine goals. At the end of the list of goals, add: "In order to …" and "In the service of …" Answer these questions allowing your unconscious to free associate—let the words fall out of your mouth. Keep repeating, "In order to …" and "In the service

182

of ..." until a word or phrase comes to you that you feel represents your mission in life. Repeat the nine goals and those two phrases ("In order to ..."; "In the service of ...") as many times as it takes. Be patient with yourself, and trust your unconscious mind. Put aside doubt, and accept what comes.

Everyone deserves self-esteem. Relating to yourself with respect, kindness, and appreciation is a fundamental human right. Why then is it so problematic? Why do so many not have it? Boundaries are absolutely necessary for self-esteem, but when you don't know what's happening to you, you're powerless to do anything about it. When you're not aware of boundaries and how to "do" them, you get stuck in the distortions of boundaries, which severely damages your relationship with yourself.

No matter what we discover in astronomy, physics, biology, psychology—all the sciences—our human life remains. No matter how many questions are answered, more questions arise. Perhaps that's the beauty of humanity—and the challenge. Looking at relationships with ourselves and others through the lens of boundaries lifts some of the fog around being together and being individual. How can I be separate and yet connected? How can I lose myself in my lover, my children, my art, my work, or nature *and* be who I am—unique and independent? I hope this idea of human boundaries and how we create and maintain them has given you food for thought and tools to use to move forward in your journey of evolution as you claim your right to self-esteem.

"Once the realization is accepted that even between the closest human beings infinite distances continue to exist, a wonderful living side by side can grow up if they succeed in loving the distance between them which makes it possible for each to see the other whole against the sky." (*Letters To A Young Poet*, Rainer Maria Rilke, 1875–1926)

Imagine you are sitting in a safe and beautiful place. The air is fresh and sweet, the sounds are calming, the sky is infinite, and your body is comfortable, light, and centered. You are in a circle of like-minded people, and the respected and trusted teacher asks each of you to imagine that deep within you is a key to the next step in your evolution. This key is the recognition and acceptance of one of four existential fears. She tells you that within each of us is a primary fear that shapes our life and molds our strengths and weaknesses. Left unrecognized it is like denying that the earth revolves around the sun—comprehension of the world would rest on false and distorted assumptions. Unacknowledged, this core fear is either walled away and denied, or without boundaries, it is diffused throughout every aspect of our life.

Identifying and accepting our primary fear creates boundaries, puts our life in perspective, and makes sense out of what was random and chaotic. It helps us to understand the road we're on and to translate the detours and traps along the way into meaningful symbols of our evolution. "Fears are the dragons guarding our most precious treasures." (*Letters To A Young Poet*, Rainer Maria Rilke, 1875–1926).

The teacher asks you to close your eyes and go deep within yourself to the place of your limitless unconscious and listen to the words she will speak—resting comfortably in the knowledge that you will recognize your primary fear when you hear it, today, tomorrow, or whenever the time is right. Respect yourself and your inner process. One of these fears is an important challenge to and messenger for your evolution. Is it the fear of death, the fear of being alone, the fear that you create your life, the fear that life has no meaning? This fear is not bad or good—it simply is and as such is not to be avoided.

Your primary fear is often buried under layers of behaviors and emotions that are limiting. Simple acknowledgment, without solving or eliminating it, creates a deeper understanding and appreciation of where you've been and how you must continue. It is a key to your relationship with yourself—your self-esteem—as you explore the boundaries of your individuality and togetherness, being separate and connected.

Once upon a time there was a blade of grass. She was in great despair; she kept being either frozen, flooded, burned by the sun, or trampled upon by hundreds of heavy shoes and boots! Just when she was beginning to be happy, stretching upward to the blue sky and warm sun, listening to the birds call to one another, and feeling the breeze caress her, she was cut down, flattened out, and pressed against the earth. Someone who did not know what he was doing cut her so short that she could hardly breathe, and she certainly could not hear the birds' songs or feel the breeze. After a few days, she noticed that she had grown a little and could begin to stretch out and look up to the sky again.

However, after a few weeks the sun burned so intensely that she lost all her beautiful green color and turned brown and dry. She thought for sure that the end was near. Just at that moment, the rain came, and she drank deeply of the cool moisture. Soon, again, she regained her color.

Something always seemed to happen to hurt her or put her in danger: the ice and snow, the hot sun, or people walking, running, and jumping on her. Life was not worth living this way!

One day a beautiful butterfly landed close by. There was something wonderful about this butterfly. The blade of grass began to talk to her and eventually told her her story of sorrow.

The butterfly was very sympathetic and began to speak. "I can understand how you feel, but I must say I am quite surprised by your story. You see, from my perspective, way up high above you in this field, I watch you day after day. I see how you are so flexible that the worst storms never break you, no matter what happens to you. Being stepped on repeatedly, being frozen or burnt—you always pick yourself up, look up, and stretch yourself high to the sky and clouds. And when the wind blows, I can hear your soft beautiful song."

The blade of grass thanked the butterfly and was quiet for a long time. Then she began to smile to herself and hum a happy song—for she at last realized that her whole life was one of success.

Suggested reading

- Bandler, R, & Grinder, J, (1989), *Structure of Magic: A Book About Language and Therapy v1*, Science and Behavior Books, Pablo Alto, CA
- Bandler, R, & Grinder, J, (1989), *Structure of Magic: V2*, Science and Behavior Books, Pablo Alto, CA
- Davis, M, & Wallbridge, D, (1991), *Boundaries and Space: An Introduction to the Work of D. W. Winnicott*, Brunner-Mazel, New York
- Linden, A, (2008), *Mindworks: An Introduction to NLP*, Crown House Publishing, Carmarthen
- Rilke, R M, (1993), *Duino Elegies*, W W Norton, New York
- Rossi, E, L, (ed), (1989), *The Collected Papers of Milton H Erickson, Vols I–IV*, Irvington Publishers Inc, New York
- Rossi, E, L, et al (ed), (1989), *Healing in Hypnosis, Vol 1 & 2 by Milton H Erickson*, Irvington Publishers Inc, New York
- Satir, V, (1972), *Peoplemaking*, Science and Behavior Books, Pablo Alto, CA
- Schwartz, R, (1995), *Internal Family Systems Therapy*, Guilford Publications, New York
- Watzlawick, P, et al (1974*), Change: Principles of Problem Foundation and Problem Resolution*, W W Norton, New York

For further information

For more information on Anné Linden's training and publications, visit the website www.nlpcenter.com or call or fax 1-845-626-2976.